Ruth the Truth's
PSYCHIC GUIDE TO FINDING LOVE

Ruth the Truth's
PSYCHIC GUIDE TO FINDING LOVE

PIATKUS

Copyright © 2002 by Ruth Urquhart

First published in 2002 by
Judy Piatkus (Publishers) Limited
5 Windmill Street
London WLT 2JA
e-mail: info@piatkus.co.uk

The moral rights of the author have been asserted

A catalogue record for this book is available from the British Library

ISBN 0–7499–2329-6

Edited by Lizzie Hutchins
Illustrations by Rodney Paull

This book has been printed on paper manufactured with respect for the environment using wood from managed sustainable resources

Typeset by Phoenix Photosetting, Chatham, Kent
Printed and bound in Great Britain by
Antony Rowe Ltd, Chippenham, Wilts

DEDICATION

This book on love is dedicated to my wee Scottish grannie, Betty Newlands, who taught me so much in such a short space of time when she was on Earth and continues to do so on the other side; to my Turkish grannie, Mumine Secmezsoy, whom I didn't meet on Earth but certainly know now in the spiritual plane; also to my Aunty May, who died far too young at the age of 57 – you never suffered fools gladly and taught me a spade is a spade. You have all helped me and still do whenever I connect with you.

CONTENTS

ACKNOWLEDGEMENTS

I want to give thanks to my sisters Ayfer and Soraya for their help in putting this book together; to my mum and dad, as without their help I would not be able to function, especially from a childcare perspective; to Bob Bird at the *Scottish News of the World*, June Smith-Sheppard at *Chat* magazine and Tracie Bunce, also at *Chat*, for all their help in making me and my columns such a success; not forgetting Peter Cox, Kay Cox, Malcolm Speed, Trevor Ward and all at the *Scottish Daily Record*; and Chris at Raven, who supplies me with crystals, herbs and oils and gives me so much valuable information on the magical world.

Piatkus gets a special mention – as my publishers they have always stood by me, especially Judy Piatkus and Philip Cotterell. I shouldn't forget Russell Evans, who planned the tour for my last book with such precision and expertise, and finally Paola Ehrlich, who made the media listen to my pearls of wisdom.

Without you all I would be nothing.

INTRODUCTION

LOVE IS, AS THEY SAY, a many-splendoured thing. Love is all around us – so many shades of love, from the love you have for a pet to the love you have for your soul mate. Love makes the world a very colourful place. Being in love makes you feel good. It gives you a warm squishy feeling, as if you had just eaten a big chocolate cake. No wonder we all want to experience it. As psychic agony aunt for *Chat* magazine and the *Scottish Daily Record*, I get loads of letters every day and the thing most people want to know about is love. That's why I'm writing this book – to give you my own special tips for finding and keeping the man of your dreams.

To help you, I will share with you my unique psychic ability and wisdom. I started to have acute psychic insight at the age of four. Since then I have learned to use my powers to help people in all walks of life. I learned so much about the psychic world from my Scottish grannie. She helped me to tame my abilities and always accepted me, no matter what. Not a day goes by that I don't wish she was here to see how well I have done. But with a tear in my eye and an ache in my heart I know she is looking down on me and bragging to all on the other side.

All my family have loved and cherished me. They are strong, slightly mad but loving people. My mother came from Hamilton in Scotland and my father from Istanbul in Turkey. He had been brought up in an orphanage and as a young man had come to Glasgow to work in the hotel trade. He fell in love, married and settled down in Scotland. Love changed the course of his life dramatically and, who knows, it may do the same for you.

When I was born my poor mother was very ill, as it had been a long and difficult labour. But on 21 August 1968 at 9.44 a.m. I came into the world and was welcomed by my family. Their love has made me the person I am today and has helped me through all the difficult times in my life. When I was young I was traumatised by bullies at school, who picked on me because I had a strange name and even stranger skills. I had a hard time accepting my skills myself. When I realised not everyone could do the things that came so naturally to me, I felt a freak and became very depressed. As it was, teachers at school were already complaining that I was scaring children with my visions and predictions.

Luckily my gran came to my rescue. She was very gifted herself. Her mother had come over to Scotland from Ireland and may have been from a Romany family. Thirty-five years before I was born my gran had been told by a fortune-teller that one of her grandchildren would have a very strong gift which would take them to every corner of the Earth to help people. She taught me how to develop my skills and how to do readings for people. She also taught me many of the love rituals I will share with you in this book.

My two younger sisters, Ayfer and Soraya, have also been my guiding lights on many occasions. When I had post-natal depression with my two children they rallied around and supported me, even though they had young families themselves. That is what families do for each other.

My gran always saw me writing for newspapers and magazines, but I initially trained as a scientist. It was not until after the birth of my daughter Jessica that I started writing features for a local paper. Later I had the idea of becoming Britain's first psychic agony aunt. By getting vibes from readers' letters and photographs I found I was able to help them through difficult times.

I am also, as far as I am aware, the only person in Britain who uses witchdoctor bones to reveal the future. These bones were given to my friend Anne by a village shaman in South Africa just before he died. He told her they were for 'her opposite far away'. Anne realised they were destined for me, her opposite in looks and height and far away in Scotland. At first I had no idea what to do with them, so I did some research into bone casting, an ancient art which is still practised by many African tribes. My bones are from the Zulu tribe. They have proved invaluable in helping me make a positive difference to people's lives – including their love lives.

The love of my own life has been my husband Ronald. Meeting him at 16 was a gateway to a wonderful adventure. Little did we know as teenagers how far we would go. We have been married for 14 years now and the love between us is stronger than ever. So many friends, families and colleagues have not gone as far, with divorces or separations being their destiny. The rituals learned in part from my Scottish, Turkish and Irish families have put me in a very strong position to keep my love alive and I now have great joy in sharing my wonderful knowledge with you.

So many friends and family members have complained that they need magical advice about relationships, a straightforward book free of confusing psychobabble. Some books make love sound mechanical, methodical and even just plain boring. But love is fun and magical – and this book is too! It is packed with everything you need to bewitch your man, harness your love energy and give yourself the best shot at finding true love.

In Chapter 1 the groundwork that you have to do to find love is explained. Just like an exam, you have to prepare first to get results. Of course finding love is much more fun than taking an exam and I will show you how to open your heart so that love has an easier chance of entering your life.

In Chapter 2 I will teach you how to attract love with rituals and learn to recognise love when it comes to you. You can even get to grips with dreaming your lover – a ritual so potent I know zillions of people it has worked for. You will also want to know if you are compatible, so I offer some ways to check this out using numerology and astrology.

Chapter 3 looks at how to survive that all-important first date. I will reveal to you my perfect date ritual to help it go without a hitch and will also look at the practical side of things such as what colour you should wear. Another vital factor is how to keep calm. Don't worry – I can show you how to stay cool as a cucumber!

Chapter 4 moves on from the first date to developing a relationship in the 21st century. Mobile phones, text messages and e-mails can all become instruments of love if you know how. Sending loving vibes via my text-message ritual is awesome and not to be missed by any cool chick out there with a mobile firmly in her hand. You can also get help from the most amazing sources – the heavens above. I will show you how to connect with your spirit guides and guardian angels. Every little thing helps.

Chapter 5 is a beautiful chapter, as it offers many pearls of wisdom on how to build your relationship, moving from a puppy dog kind of love to something more intense and spiritual, a true meeting of hearts and souls. I will explain to you how to do a ritual to celebrate your love and how to find common interests and develop this important part of your relationship.

Chapter 6 is where we get hot under the collar with the subject of sex – not just the hanky panky, but ways to make your sex life a more spiritual one, which will in turn make it more enjoyable and longer lasting. I will reveal to you a beautiful lovers' ritual my Scottish gran taught me. Of course I will also look at aphrodisiacs and how they can help your love life go more smoothly. I will show you how to be a goddess in and out of bed, so make sure you are ready with a cold bucket of water or, better still, a cold shower!

My final chapter is probably my favourite. It is my Love Oracle – a special little present to you, my reader. Just between you and me, I have charged it up with my positive powers and you can use it to ask questions about your love life. I have had many people tell me how amazingly accurate it is and it has a special message for every single person who consults it. I will reveal how to make it work for you.

My book is written with love about love. May it take you on the journey of a lifetime to find love.

Many blessings,
Ruth

WHAT YOU WILL NEED . . .

THERE IS NOTHING WORSE than coming across a brilliant ritual in a book only to discover that you don't have the ingredients, or bits and bobs as I call them, to do it properly. The following is a list of all the things you will need to carry out all the fabulous rituals you will read about in this book. There is some advice, too, about the timing of rituals.

CANDLES

Candles are used in many of my rituals as they give beautiful soft lighting and fire is an important spiritual element. The colour of the candles is important as it reflects the purpose behind the ritual, so for example pink candles are used for romantic love and red ones for passion. The colours you will need are:

Blue For healing

Green For rituals concerning the heart and communication with guardian angels

Orange To signify the power of the Sun

Pink For romantic love

Red For passion and strength

White For acceptance and communication with spirit guides

Yellow For lifting the spirits

HERBS, ESSENTIAL OILS AND INCENSE

HERBS

Herbs are used in many of my rituals, as they have their own magical properties. They have been harnessed by the power of nature which helped them to grow and have many and varied uses, including curing ailments and illness as well as making rituals work.

The herbs you will need to have to hand are:

Basil (fresh)

Camomile (fresh or dried)

Dill (fresh or dried)

Rosemary (fresh or dried)

Thyme (fresh or dried)

ESSENTIAL OILS

Essential oils come from aromatic plants such as lavender and basil. They can be used in an oil burner to give a pleasant aroma to the room in which you are performing your ritual. The aromas will also help you to concentrate your thoughts. I use essential oils to help my rituals work, as generations of my family have done before me.

The essential oils you will need are:

Geranium
Jasmine
Lavender
Musk
Patchouli
Rose
Sandalwood
Vanilla
Ylang ylang

INCENSE

Incense is also burned to enhance the senses and it is associated with the elements of air and fire, the air being represented by the smoke and the fire by the burning ash. Incense helps to keep you grounded during a ritual and it can protect you from negative forces.

The incenses you will need:

Amber
Cinnamon
Frankincense
Rose
Sage (smudge stick)
Vanilla

CRYSTALS

I use crystals all the time in my rituals as they are like small stores of energy which help to activate the magic. I see them almost as batteries which make the whole system work. Each crystal has a different energy and is therefore used in working different rituals. For example, rose quartz has a vibration associated with the heart so it is used in love rituals. The crystals I use are the small, stone-sized ones. You can buy them from retail outlets or by mail order. I get all my crystals from a great mail-order company called Raven and their address is at the back of the book.

The crystals you should have at the ready are:

Amethyst
Aventurine
Citrine quartz
Clear quartz
Lapis lazuli
Lodestone
Pink tourmaline
Rose quartz
Turquoise

OTHER ITEMS

It will be useful to have red, pink, yellow, gold and white ribbon to hand as well as string in a whole array of colours.
Pens and paper will also be helpful so that you can be ready to bring some art into your magic. You will need blue,

red, green and white pens, white, pink and black paper and pink and orange card.

THE PHASES OF THE MOON

The Moon is a powerful instrument in making your rituals and charms work. It helps to energise them with its power. It has four main phases, which have specific energies:

Waxing Moon This is when the Moon is progressing towards full illumination. This phase will help attract something to you, such as love or money.

Full Moon This is when the Moon is fully illuminated. It is the most powerful phase of all and brings with it expansion of projects and ideas. It also helps with matters of fertility and love which need a little help to grow.

Waning Moon This is when the Moon's illumination is decreasing after a Full Moon. If you want to get rid of something or let go of emotions such as jealousy, then this is the Moon to work by. It will move things away from you.

New Moon This is when there is no Moon to be seen in the sky. The first day of the New Moon is great for rituals to bring new things into your life. The second day is a day of rest, and magic or rituals should be avoided then.

PROTECTION

The most important thing when you are doing rituals is to feel safe and secure. You can always protect yourself before doing any magical work by closing your eyes and imagining you are immersed in golden light from head to toe, with the light coming from the universe above. This will mean that you have a shield stopping negativity from entering your domain. Then you can open your eyes and do your work.

When you have finished your ritual, do the same thing in reverse – just close your eyes and turn the light off. Open your eyes and you are ready to go about your normal business.

Once you are confident in doing the rituals and exercises I give here, you will be able to make up your own. So always keep a notebook handy for jotting down ideas as they come along.

Rituals are a great way of achieving things you want in life. Have faith in your abilities and you will get results. Just look at me and see how they have helped me to achieve my goals.

Have a great, fun and enchanting time.

Chapter 1
PREPARING TO ACCEPT LOVE

NO MATTER WHAT STAGE you have reached in your life, if you want to find someone special to love and to be loved in return you need to prepare for it. How can you expect the love of your life to arrive unless you are ready to receive love? First you have to accept who you are and break free from the chains of the past. This chapter will show you how. Preparation is the key to your success, so enjoy it.

OPEN YOUR HEART!

We can't see love, but we can feel it. It comes from the heart. The heart has been considered the focus of love since time immemorial and to prepare for love you need to open your heart. The way to do this is to work with the heart chakra (*see* illustration, page 14). *Chakra* is an Indian word meaning 'energy centre'. There are seven of these in the body. Each has a particular job to do and the one in the heart area lets love enter and grow in our lives. I want to show you how to work on this chakra, massage it and open it up.

If you have ever suffered a broken relationship, an abusive one or just an unhappy one, your heart will have taken a battering and your heart chakra will have closed up. I remember as a 13 year old meeting the most wonderful guy at a Young Socialists meeting. He was 18 and a student at Edinburgh University. He turned out to be my first boyfriend and I really loved him in a teenage way. But after three years together we parted and it broke my heart. I felt that my world had been torn apart and that I would never smile again. Then I remembered that my grannie had

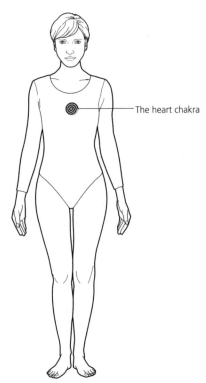

The heart chakra

The heart chakra.

told me that I would meet the man I would marry at 16 and indeed I did – my sweetheart Ronald. If you've had your heart broken, you will feel sore emotionally and spiritually, but learning to open your heart chakra will allow the healing process to begin and love to enter your life again.

Opening the Heart Chakra

You will need:
* Green candle
* Vanilla incense

This is a very important exercise, so either tape yourself reading it out loud or, if you have an excellent memory, memorise it.

Sit comfortably in a room in which you feel safe and secure. Make sure that you will not be disturbed for the next 10 minutes.

Take a green candle, as this is the colour signifying the heart chakra, and light it. As you do this I want you to think about how you feel when you are in love. Feel the joy that is love. You can smile if you want, or laugh. Whatever emotions you feel, just let them out.

Next I want you to light some vanilla incense. Enjoy its soothing sweet aroma. As it curls around the room let it add to your sensual enjoyment.

Now close your eyes and imagine that your heart is pumping positive red blood all around your body, giving you life and allowing you to breathe.

Then think of a brilliant green forest with tall trees and luscious foliage all around you – the most vivid green you can imagine. Feel happy that you are filled with love. Sit in your green forest and just allow nature to wash over you.

After around two minutes, begin to bring yourself back to the present day. Open your eyes and feel happy that your heart is now ready to accept the possibility of love.

————————*————————

I do this exercise myself whenever I feel low and it always gives me a positive energy boost. Whenever you are feeling sad or let down it is great at helping you to see love in all its glory. Recently a vile poison-pen letter was sent to one of my columns and I needed to reconnect with the love I receive from my clients and readership. Doing this ritual helped to get me back on track. It is a very powerful tool to have.

When you are preparing for love, I would do this exercise once a week to enrich and strengthen your heart. By thinking these positive thoughts you will create positive energy around you in your life. You will smile more and see the beauty in the most everyday things, such as a flower blooming by the side of the road. You will notice the wonder in life itself.

LEARN TO LOVE YOURSELF FIRST

To bring love into your life, the place to start is with yourself. If you don't love yourself, how is anybody else going to love you? If you don't like yourself or you feel you are worthless, then you will get that back in the relationships you develop. Remember the old adage 'Like attracts like'? You need to love yourself, warts and all, inside and out. Being positive about yourself will bring you so many rewards.

When I worked with single mothers I was always perplexed by how negative they could be about themselves. The following is the plan I got them to work through and the results were amazing. Get to grips with this and you will feel better too.

———— * ————

Learn to Appreciate Yourself

Take a minute or two to think about what a great person you are and what great things you have done – perhaps you helped an old lady to cross the road recently or helped out a family member in some way. I picked my mum up after work on a wet day, for example. I want you to put pen to paper and write down at least 10 positive things you have done, both for yourself and for others.

Once you have done this, take a few moments to look at what you have written. Just look at your list and reflect on how good you are to yourself and to other people.

Then put a value on your head. It need not be a numerical figure, but reflect values that you possess within yourself. For example my value is in the love and compassion I have for the human race.

Remember that you are a good person who deserves the best in life. Now give yourself a well-earned pat on the back.

Get a green candle, which reflects your own inner wisdom, and light it. Repeat the following incantations:

'I accept I am a blessed human being.'
'I appreciate the role I play in the world.'
'I feel I deserve to be happy.'

Do this regularly so you don't forget how utterly fabulous you are.

———— * ————

I remember doing a workshop on having a positive image and a woman came up to me after it to tell me that in all her 25 years of life she had never been able to look at herself in a mirror and be content with what she saw. She told me that as soon as she got home she would list her 10 positive things and then light a green candle. As always, I instructed her to tell me the outcome of the ritual. Seven weeks later she sent me a letter telling me that instead of 10 positive things, she had come up with 21. She realised what a cherished and well-loved person she was, and she was glad to inform me that she was no longer scared of mirrors.

LEARN TO LOVE YOUR BODY

So many of us nowadays have serious hang-ups about the way we look. It could be you don't like the shape of your nose or you think your bum is too big. Such preoccupations are a reflection of the times. Magazines bombard us with images of undernourished teenagers who keep their skin-and-bone figures in check with a diet of fags and coffee. Television is no better; I have noticed that actresses are getting tinier and tinier. Instead of trying to live up to unrealistic images we need to love our bodies, as it is through them we will meet the people who will make our lives whole. If you are negative about your appearance, this can limit love.

You need to learn to accept your body and love it for the very miracle it is. There are four things you need to do:

1. Accept that you are attractive.

2. Have a healthy life.

3. Love your body, warts and all.

4. Make positive changes if necessary – if you are genuinely unhappy about an aspect of your body, then change it if possible or make the best of it. Making positive changes to your body will make you feel more positive.

ACCEPT THAT YOU ARE ATTRACTIVE

To be successful in finding love you need to be confident. Confident people get noticed. Why not imagine that you are a goddess such as Venus?

---------*---------

Become a Goddess

Look through a magazine or book depicting a wise and mystical woman or, better still, a goddess.

Now sit comfortably and look at the picture. Take in the colours in front of you. What colour are the goddess's hair, her clothes, her eyes? What would you feel like wearing the same clothes? Imagine the feel of her skin and the warmth of her breath. Allow her energy to radiate within you.

You may feel more feminine or sexy doing this. Just go with the feelings which come to you as you tune in to your goddess image. Allow her strength to seep through your every pore.

Before you know it you will exude sexuality and find that life is full of exciting possibilities. You will accept that you look great and that you have an effect on all who meet you.

Do this simple ritual at least once every two months and do it on a Full Moon, which will give it added oomph!

———— * ————

HAVE A HEALTHY LIFE

If you are living a healthy, well-balanced life then you will feel a better person. You are also less likely to be ill and miss out on that important date you had planned or the chance of going out and meeting your soul mate.

To stay healthy and fit for love, enjoy a well-balanced diet with plenty of greens to feed your heart chakra (green is the colour related to the heart chakra), sleep well – at least eight hours are recommended – and exercise as much as you can. This will keep you ready for love action when it comes your way.

There are many psychic tools that you can use to help you maintain tip-top health, such as crystals, colour therapy and healing.

Crystals for Health

When you just don't feel right but can't put your finger on it, turquoise and clear quartz will help you to feel better. Their healing energies are great for making you feel happier within yourself. When I am feeling out of sorts, I just lie on my bed with the clear quartz in my right hand and the turquoise in my left hand.

There are also times when you will feel unhappy. Your emotions may be unbalanced. Crystals radiate energy which can sort this out for you. The best crystals to use are a combination of citrine quartz, clear quartz and amethyst. These work together to clear emotional stress.

Colour Therapy

I love colour. Anyone who has ever seen me at any of my talks can vouch for this. Colour has the ability to alter your mood for the better. So if you are feeling ill or run down, cover yourself with red or pink, or wear these colours, as they not only give you energy but also lift your spirits. I have a pink cover I drape over myself every month when I have my womanly thingys and I just feel the energy radiating through my body, making me feel better.

Healing

Healing in whatever form, whether it is spiritual, Reiki or massage, will help you balance your health. Reiki is a Japanese form of healing that can be learned by anyone. The healing energy comes from a source in the universe. I did a Reiki 1 course last year and the energy surge I felt from it was awesome. I have Reiki once a month to help me feel emotionally stable.

Healing of all sorts is great for a happy, healthy life, which in turn can lead to a happy, healthy love life.

LOVE YOUR BODY, WARTS AND ALL

I always think that this sounds like some self-help tripe, but when you think about it, having a positive body image is really important. Have you been brave enough to look at yourself in the mirror recently? I have. OK, so I am a big girl with lots of lumps and bumps, but I still have a positive attitude about my body. And let's face it, if I can't learn to love my body, why should anyone else? None of us is perfect, but it is a joy that we are all different sizes, shapes and colours.

If you are feeling low about the way you look, try this great ritual.

————*————

Loving Your Body

You will need:
* White candle
* Amethyst
* Fresh thyme

The white candle signifies acceptance. Light it and with your right hand (whether you are left or right-handed), hold the crystal as near to your heart as possible. The amethyst will encourage positive thoughts. The thyme can sit directly in front of you. This is good for concentration.

Now sit quietly, close your eyes and say the following with great meaning and emotion:

'I love my body, warts and all.
My body is a temple.
It keeps me alive and well.'

This is a powerful affirmation I learned from a healer I met on a psychic development workshop I ran a couple of years ago. It helps you focus on your body as a positive entity. Just read it out to yourself and feel inspired instantly! Come on, you believe it!

———— * ————

MAKE POSITIVE CHANGES

Now let's get down to improving your appearance. Can you sit here today and pinpoint what you don't like about it? Look at the following and see what changes could be made.

Image

What does your image say about you? Will it attract the opposite sex? Ask your friends for their honest advice. Is it up to date? Get ideas from books or fashion magazines, but make sure you don't become a fashion victim. It can easily happen. If you are feeling stuck for inspiration, do this easy ritual. With a little help from it, you will find your own unique style.

———— * ————

Asking for Image Inspiration

You will need:
* Green candle
* Rose incense
* Green ink or a green pen
* White paper

Do this on a Friday, as this day is ruled by Venus, goddess of beauty.

First burn some rose incense. Rose is the scent associated with this goddess. Then light your candle and just sit quietly and ask Venus to give you guidance on your image.

Next write your request in green ink on white paper and place it under your pillow when you go to sleep. You will either dream of what direction to take with your image or you will be inspired in the morning.

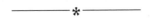

I did this simple ritual when I was 22, as my fashion sense was sad and wacky. I dreamed that I was in a shop buying more fashionable clothes. Let's see what you are inspired to do.

Hair

Does your mane let you down? Is the style old-fashioned? A good cut, colour and conditioner will make all the difference to how you feel. My Scottish grannie was amazing in her knowledge of herbs and she told me that if you have dull hair a great way to liven it up is with a rinse of fresh rosemary leaves.

———— * ————

Rosemary Rinse

You will need:
* Rosemary leaves
* Water
* Washed-out shampoo bottle or any other kind of bottle

Fill the washed-out shampoo bottle with fresh tap water, add some fresh rosemary leaves and put it in the fridge for 24 hours. Wash your hair as usual and give it a final rinse with the rosemary rinse. Brush out the rosemary leaves and see the difference it makes to your crowning glory!

———————— * ————————

I had the best hair in my street, all because of my grannie.

Skin

You want your skin to look good, too, and plenty of water and a good moisturiser will make all the difference. I have moisturised since I was 20 and I think I have pretty good skin for a 34 year old. An old remedy my grannie taught me for tired skin is this oatmeal face scrub.

———————— * ————————

Oatmeal Face Scrub

You will need:
* 100 ml (3.5 fl oz) fresh water
* 200 g (7 oz) fine oatmeal

Mix the water and the oatmeal together in a bowl and then place the mixture on your skin, wash in a circular motion and rinse it all off. The oatmeal acts as a natural exfoliator, removing all dead skin cells and allowing skin renewal to take place. Your skin will be left soft and bright.

———————— * ————————

Weight

Exercise and a healthy diet will help you to keep this within a healthy range. If you want natural help, then look to the Sun, as that governs our health concerns, and if you are really serious about losing weight do the following ritual.

———————*———————

To Lose Weight

You will need:
* Orange candle
* Cinnamon incense

Do this ritual on a Sunday, as the Sun rules this day.

Light the candle and then burn the incense. Both the orange candle and the cinnamon represent the Sun and its wonderful healing power.

Sit quietly and imagine that you are the weight you want to be. Just think about how wonderful you feel and how your health has improved.

Ask the Sun to give you the determination and will-power to lose weight.

———————*———————

A friend of mine did this and lost two stone so that she could fit into her bikini on holiday.

Making these positive improvements to your body can be a lot of fun. I often have my friends over so we can do beauty treatments on each other. The feeling of sisterhood helps us to feel good and part of a really important group. And of course we look fabulous too!

LEARN TO LOVE YOUR MIND

Now I want you to prepare your mind so that others will see you for the interesting person you are. You really are worth knowing and if you think so you will radiate a positive feeling about yourself which will be infectious, so people will be drawn to you. Remember, any possible soul mate will want to be with someone with a positive attitude about themselves – a fun person, not a sour puss.

I have done lots of work on TV and I once met an actor who in real life was as gorgeous as the character he played on screen. He asked me if I could have a private word with him after our interviews were over. I said, 'Yes, of course,' and was so chuffed he wanted to speak to me. I had just sat down in the private office set aside for our meeting when he broke down crying. 'I feel ugly and stupid and can never find a girl who is on my wavelength,' he said with his head in his arms. Quick as a flash I said to him that his wavelength at present was 'Relationship Failure', as he had such a negative opinion of himself. I gave him the four pearls of wisdom I am about to share with you and recently I saw a picture of him arm in arm with a beautiful actress in a celebrity magazine. So I guess it worked for him.

These four points are not rocket science, but very simple:

1. Learn to love yourself.

2. Be positive.

3. Find happiness in yourself.

4. Harness your self-confidence.

LEARN TO LOVE YOURSELF

We've already looked at learning to love your body. Part of loving your mind is to be aware of your accomplishments throughout your life. Every day you achieve more. Have you ever taken the time to sit down and think about what you have achieved, from school to college or university and at work and within your family? I bet you haven't, so let's do it now. This will help you to realise just how special you really are.

As you are so special, you deserve to be treated well – you are a goddess, after all, and they never expect anything less. Allow your inner goddess to guide you in all you do. She always gets it right. Your inner goddess is the female spirit which lies within all women. She is there to help us and give us wisdom in all that we do in our lives.

———*———

Connecting with Your Inner Goddess

To help you connect with your inner goddess, close your eyes and imagine that you are on top of a mountain, sitting on a wooden seat.

Next to you is your inner goddess. Your inner wisdom will tell you what she looks like. Speak to her about how you are feeling and listen to her wise words.

When you feel she has helped you sufficiently, thank her and make your way down the mountain. To make this easier I just get a cable car to the bottom. It is an amazing experience and I love doing it.

Once you are down, slowly open your eyes and reconnect with the here and now.

———*———

BE POSITIVE

Are you the type of person who is always waiting for things to go wrong? Or do you see the shortcomings in people instead of the good things they can do? If so, it is likely that you have a negative view of life. Also, if you are critical of yourself, you tend to be critical of others, because you judge them by the high standards you set for yourself.

You can't possibly expect beautiful pure love to enter your life if you have a negative attitude. So dump it right now. Here are six great ways to embrace the positive.

1. Be Philosophical

Your first step towards being positive is to understand that things can't always be great. Life can really suck at times, but what is important is the way you react and get through those times. The best way is to look at the great things you can learn from a negative experience and relish the good times when they eventually return!

2. Talk Positive

Use positive words to describe yourself, words like 'I am', 'I will', 'I can' and 'I shall' instead of 'I can't', 'I might', 'I shan't'. Just try this and see how positive you feel.

3. Surround Yourself with Positive People

It's frightening how catching bad vibes can be. So often I would be full of the joys of spring and then a negative friend would pop into my home and negativity would reign supreme. I call these people 'emotional vampires' as they suck you dry, leaving you down in the dumps. So make sure you surround yourself with positive people and keep emotional vampires at bay!

4. Block Negative Thoughts

Each time you feel a negative thought coming into your mind, close your eyes and imagine the thought going into a large metal bin. Then, with great force, put a lid on it. Only allow positive thoughts into your mind. That way you will welcome positive things, happier things, as the norm.

5. Look on Each Problem as a Challenge

A problem is only an opportunity to learn and expand your experience. Be enthusiastic about whatever life has to throw at you. Remember:

Problem = Challenge

A great example I have of this is when I was sacked from the *Evening Times* in Glasgow after six years. I just walked out and went straight over to ask the *News of the World* for a job. I could have gone home and cried, but my challenge was to show the editor who had sacked me that I could do better for myself. And I did. Challenges are fun, problems never are.

6. Use Your 'Mind Magnet'

You have the power within you to attract both the positive and the negative, just as if your mind were a magnet. So you can use your 'mind magnet' to banish negative thoughts and make positive ones stick.

———— * ————

Activating Your 'Mind Magnet'

Find a room you can feel comfortable in. Then sit down and make sure your feet can rest firmly on the ground. It is important to be grounded for this exercise.

Then close your eyes and imagine that you are surrounded by positive white light covering the whole of your body so that you are glowing from top to bottom. This is your positive magnetic shield. It is there to protect you from anything negative. Negative thoughts, vibes or energy from other people will not get through your white light shield. This in turn will activate your mind magnet and positive thoughts and energy will be drawn to you.

You can now open your eyes and after you have taken a moment to come to, you can go about your daily business.

If you ever want to deactivate your mind magnet at any time, all you have to do is sit at peace again and close your eyes. Then imagine that you have a switch on top of your head you can use to turn off the white light. Open your eyes and there you are.

———— * ————

FIND HAPPINESS IN YOURSELF

Think back to a time when you were in the company of a happy person. Didn't they make you feel good too? Happy people radiate a feel-good factor. If you get the happy bug then people will be drawn to you and it will really help your chances of finding love. Just decide from today that you are Miss Happy and that you will 'smile your way around the day'. See what a difference it makes.

Here are five simple steps to happiness:

1. Think Happy

Whatever the circumstances in your life, react in a positive way. For example, say you lose your job. If you are looking at this from a negative point of view, you will be found sitting with your head in your hands, wondering what on Earth will happen next. If you have your happy hat on, then you will see this as an opportunity to start something better and more fulfilling. Think happy to be happy.

2. Talk Happy

The simplest way to think happy is to use a mantra. A mantra is a devotional incantation. Buddhists and Hindus use them in their prayers. A mantra helps to concentrate your thoughts on a single subject close to your heart, so it is a great way to change your feelings to the way you want them to be.

To be happy, just tell yourself: 'I am happy. Yes, I am really, really happy.' This is your new mantra. Say it as many times as you like during the day. Go on, just see how great it leaves you feeling.

3. Stop Seeking Approval

Happy souls never need to ask people for approval, as they are comfortable in their own skins. Accept yourself for the loving human being you are.

4. Accept Yourself and Your Abilities

If you are happy you can genuinely look in the mirror and look back at yourself with a smile. No hang-ups, no pangs of sadness, just happiness. As I have said to you before, I am a big girl, but I never look at myself and think, 'Oh my God, how fat are you?!', I just say, 'Wow, how are you doing, Gorgeous?' Accept the way things are and not the way you think they should be. You will find life treats you a whole lot better and in a crowded room people will be attracted to your happy aura.

5. Enjoy Today

My grannie always used to say to me that this is not a rehearsal, it is the real deal. So don't dig into the past and think about what you might have done. That is a real waste of time. Enjoy each day as if it were your last and life will feel better. Also, don't worry about what might happen, as this can never improve your situation. Learn from the past and enjoy what today has to offer you.

I know you are feeling happier and more content already. Life is getting better and love is just around the corner!

HARNESS YOUR SELF-CONFIDENCE

If you are confident, you will discover that people will find you alluring. This because someone who is self-assured makes others feel safe and secure.

Here are my four ways to become more confident. They really do work – just look at how well I have done. I think my confidence has grown out of necessity, because people, especially in the media, want to put psychics down all the time. If I didn't have confidence in myself and my abilities I would never have made it as far as I have.

1. Encourage Feelings of Self-worth

Take time to reflect as before on everything you have achieved in your life. Believe wholeheartedly that you are a beautiful being worthy of all the joys that life can bring. You have a valued place on this planet. You are the only person who can determine what you are worth, so don't shortchange yourself. If you do make a mistake or do something you are not proud of, just put it down to experience and move on.

A great ritual for self-confidence is one my great-aunt taught me when I was studying for exams at school. She told me to take a photo of myself and put it in a red envelope and then put the envelope inside my pillowcase. I woke up the next day feeling much more positive about myself and the exams I had to take. When I asked my great-aunt why this had happened she told me that red was the colour of strength and positivity. The fact I had an image of myself in a red envelope had activated my feelings of self-worth. It was that simple.

2. Don't Put Yourself Down

This is certainly one I can put my hand up to. I am always making jokes about my weight and I guess that I just do it to make people feel OK with me. My family gets really cross with me about this, especially my sisters Ayfer and Soraya. Putting yourself down does nothing to enhance your image but much to damage it. So don't do it, not even in a jokey way. If you want someone to love you then you need to have a positive image of yourself. This is the first step to a confident new you.

3. Accept a Compliment

In Britain it is so unacceptable to accept a compliment. I don't know why this should be, but we need to act as a nation to stop it. Look at the Americans; we could really learn a thing or two from them. They take compliments and accept them in the way they were given.

Think about the last time someone said you looked good or had cooked a great meal. Did you accept it or did you just say something along the lines of 'Not at all' or 'No, I am looking awful today'? Next time you get a compliment, thank the person for giving it to you. Accept that it is a positive thing. Accept compliments and you will see your self-esteem soar.

4. Believe You Are More Confident Than You Really Are

Acting confidently will allow you to experience what it is like. So be a great actress!

A great way to do this is to go to the supermarket dressed up to the nines – make-up on, clothes that show your curves and heels to die for. Imagine you are starring in a film and the cameras are rolling. Then, as you are going up and down the food aisle, spot a lone male, preferably cute with tight buns. Well, that would be my preference if I were single! Slink over to him, walking with a sexy shimmy, and ask him if he knows where the milk cabinet is, making sure you make eye contact and get his attention.

You will feel great, I can guarantee it, and next time you can cut the act and just be your confident self.

Now that you are getting your mind and body ready for love, you need to learn to heal yourself of the past so that you can connect with the future.

HEALING YOURSELF OF PAST HURTS

Whatever your experiences are now and whatever your past experiences have been, you will have baggage from past relationships. One of the sure-fire ways to continued relationship failure is not to resolve past conflicts. You may just carry on as if things were fine, but the past will catch up with you sooner or later and your inner turmoil will reveal itself. You need to accept the past and heal yourself to be ready for the possibilities that a new relationship will bring.

Take some time just now to think about the disappointment, hurt, sadness and disillusionment you may have suffered in the past. I suggest you do this over a two-day period, but you may need less or more time. Use your intuition to gauge it. Allow yourself to feel the emotions that arise. I know that it isn't easy to do, but trust me, you will feel better for it.

Now do the following ritual. My grannie told me about it once after I had a terrible row with Ronald and we had said really hurtful things to each other. I was sure that it was the end of the relationship, but after I did the ritual, I felt much better and was ready to forgive my future husband. I still carry it out to this day whenever I am feeling battered and bruised after an argument with a friend or family member. It is a simple ritual, but it will allow you to put the past behind you once and for all.

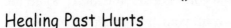

Healing Past Hurts

You will need:
* Access to running water – a stream, the sea, a tap or shower
* Piece of smooth rose quartz, about the size of a 10p coin
* Sheet of white paper
* Blue pen
* Elastic band

This may take time, so don't do it when you have a busy day ahead of you. Find a quiet, peaceful time.

Sit comfortably, take the rose quartz and hold it in both hands. Then hold it to your heart chakra. Close your eyes and repeat the following incantation:

> *'Dear Goddess,*
> *I ask you to fill this rose quartz with all the hurt I have*
> *felt in the past, all the baggage I carry from relationships*
> *which have not worked for whatever reason.*
> *I offer this crystal filled with the element of water.'*

Take the crystal and hold it under flowing water. Water has cleansing properties not just on the surface but energetically too. Therefore it allows negative past experiences to be rinsed away at a deep inner level.

Now take the paper and write down all the negative feelings you want to be banished from your life. Using a pen with blue ink signifies healing.

Wrap the crystal with the paper and secure it with the elastic band. Then take it and bury it in a natural setting at least a mile away from your house. You don't want the negativity to be kept within your living space. I can assure you that once you bury this you will feel a real weight off your mind.

————————— * —————————

Banish Past Fears

We have all had experiences which we would rather not have to go through again. In some cases we may be frightened of history repeating itself. This could build up barriers which could stop you from meeting the right person for you.

So many people write to me every week to ask me how they will ever be able to love again after being hurt by a bad relationship. It takes so much time and energy to recover. The following is a ritual I do for people who need help to release their fears of the past repeating itself in some way. It will allow you to move forward in your life and look at things in a whole new positive light. It is so straightforward to do and it will only take 10 minutes of your time, but the effects can last forever and be quite dramatic. I know people who have done this ritual and you can actually see facial lines disappearing due to the stress which has been lifted from them.

———————*———————

Fight Fear

You will need:
* Camomile (either fresh or dried)
* Blue candle
* Bowl of clear tap water
* Wooden spoon

The Moon's phase is very important in this ritual. Please note that it should be carried out during the waning phase, when the Moon is decreasing in size.

This ritual can be carried out either outside or inside, it is totally up to you. See what your intuition tells you to do.

On the night of a waning Moon, take the blue candle and light it. Think about what you fear most in having another relationship. Is it the hurt you have felt before or could it be the fact you find it difficult to trust someone or that you fear rejection? Just let your mind drift to these thoughts. It doesn't matter how you feel – in fact the more sore the better, as the healing process will work more efficiently.

Take the camomile and place it in the bowl of water.

Now, stirring the water with the wooden spoon, repeat the following:

> *'Camomile, calm my fear.*
> *Let me love for another year.*
> *Allow love to be so clear.'*

Close your eyes and feel the fear leave your life. The camomile has calming qualities which allow fear to subside, while the blue candle represents healing and its light the possibility that you can see light at the end of your dark tunnel.

————————— * —————————

I have a friend whose husband came home one night and told her that he was in love with another woman. She had two small children and was beside herself with pain and hurt. After a couple of months I directed her to do this ritual and the change in her was amazing. She realised that her marriage hadn't been as good as she had led herself to believe and she felt that the hurt was now in the past. Two years later she is happily married, this time to a guy who worships the ground she walks on. There is hope for you too, so do the ritual and see the change it can make to your heart.

HOW TO START BRINGING LOVE INTO YOUR LIFE

I believe that love and affection eventually come to those who wait and I want you to believe that too. It helps if you show love and affection to those closest to you, your family. Give out love and you will find that the world gives you love right back. I find that in my work as a psychic the more of my positive energy I give out, the more people send me love and positive wishes.

I once did a reading for a 48-year-old woman who had never been told she was loved, neither as a child nor as an adult. In her 15 years of marriage she had never told her husband she loved him and he had never told her he loved her. I know you're thinking, 'How bizarre!' I told her that from that day forward she should show at least one piece of affection to her husband a day. It would feel strange at first, but she would get used to it. Eighteen months later I met her again and her relationship was completely different. Her husband now openly showed her affection.

In my family we tell each other we love them all the time. I guess it is a very Turkish thing. I also cuddle and hug people, whether I have known them for 10 minutes or 10 years. One of my favourite things is my four-year-old son Thomas wrapping his arms around me and saying, 'I love you, Mummy.' Oh, it warms my heart and keeps me positive! So start by loving your family – all of them, even the ones you don't see eye to eye with. It will make you feel better. Just slip in an 'I love you' when you can and see what you get in return.

Now I do understand that not all of us get on with our families or they may have passed on. If so, you can just as easily show your friends you love them instead.

Here are my four ways to bring more love into the home and family:

1. Have a happy family Sunday dinner. Invite your family round for dinner and talk about old times and look at old photos or video recordings. Remember your family's happy past and use the feelings to bring happiness into the present.

2. As a family, relive a day trip you went on. For me it would be a happy day trip to Ayr when I was a little girl. Go back on that day trip, either by recalling the trip or

actually going back to the same place if that is possible. Connect with the past and it will help you to reconnect with your loved ones.

3. Write a letter or card explaining how you feel about your family and let them read it. This is an easy way of showing your true emotions.

4. Set aside time once a month to connect with your whole family. Even if you live far away, you can all agree to light a white candle at the same time each day of each month, for example the last Thursday of every month at 9 p.m. This could be your quiet time to reflect on the love you feel for your family. It works over a distance, so there are no excuses. Just light the candle and as you watch the flame flicker, send a message of love and hope to all your family.

Bringing love into the home and family will make you feel better and put you on course to find the love you want.

HELP FROM YOUR HIGHER SELF AND SPIRIT HELPERS

Now I know you're thinking, 'What is this woman on about, Higher Self?' By your Higher Self I mean your spiritual self, your soul, your inner voice. Connecting with this part of yourself makes it easier to go on to connect with your spirit guides, guardian angels or goddess. You can think of these as your special assistants who help you on life's journey.

To connect with your Higher Self or soul, all you need to do is to learn to be still, relax and meditate. In the busy lives we lead today this can sometimes be very difficult, but it is worth taking the time to do it before you carry on. It is also important to understand that you won't be able to connect with your Higher Self immediately or speak to your helpers. It will take time and practice, so be patient.

Connecting with Your Higher Self

I want you to lie on your bed and make sure you are cosy and warm. Place your hands by your sides and close your eyes.

Imagine you are walking up a hill at quite a steady pace. As you get higher and higher, imagine you can see a beautiful panoramic view emerging.

As you get to the top of the hill, a little out of puff but feeling well, you can see for miles. The sun is shining and life feels good.

On top of the hill, imagine you can speak to a part of yourself that is your Higher Self. You may sense its presence in some way – perhaps an image might come into your mind, or you might hear an inner voice, or you might get a gut feeling.

Loved ones who have passed on, your guardian angels and spirit guides can also come to see you as you are at such a great height. You will know that they are there as they will appear to you or you will hear their voices. Your loved ones might speak to you as if they have never been away. You will feel at one with nature and at one with your spirit.

Once you have finished your chat you can say goodbye and walk back down the hill.

As you get to the bottom, become aware of your surroundings and feel the bed you are lying on. Then open your eyes and be happy that you now know how to contact your Higher Self.

The exercise you have just carried out will have done two things: it will have helped you connect with your Higher Self and helped you develop a communication with your guides. Your Higher Self is always there for you and your guides are with you even if you are not aware of their presence. Once you have begun to connect with them, you may feel that someone is watching you or feel a draught pass by with no explanation. That will be your guides, so learn to read the signs they give you.

Now you can use this knowledge to connect with your helpers individually. You may find your spirit guides speak the most sense or that your guardian angels look after you really well or that your goddess helps out in ways no one else can.

CONNECTING WITH YOUR SPIRIT GUIDES

When we die I believe – in fact I have seen proof – that we go on to another world which I call the spiritual realm. Here the dead live fulfilling lives as they did when they were alive, or they can come back to the Earth plane, where we are, to help us out as spirit guides.

We all have spirit guides. I have two main ones, my gran and my friend Anna, who passed away with cancer at just 46 years of age. My grannie died of cancer too, but at 81, and she had always had an active life. Although they have passed over, these people guide me in death as they did in life and normally, as long as I listen to them, things are OK. A spirit guide doesn't have to be a relative of yours; it can be a friend or just someone from the other side who connects with you.

To connect with your spirit guides is very simple. You can use the same guided imagery you use to connect with your Higher Self, or you can try my five-point plan given in Chapter 4 (*see page 133*), or you can do the following ritual:

———————*———————

Asking Your Spirit Guides for Help

You will need:
* White candle

Sit quietly and concentrate on the flame of a white candle.

As you look at the candle, ask your spirit guides to help you in your quest for love.

You may get a sign such as the candle flame flickering or a draught on your neck. I have known people to sense a comforting pat on the back. This is your spirit guides letting you know that they are there for you.

———————*———————

Your spirit guides can help you make decisions which can make the difference between meeting Mr Right and missing him. You normally don't know that they are acting on your behalf, but just accept that they are and go with your instincts, as these are your guides' way of helping you.

CONNECTING WITH YOUR GUARDIAN ANGELS

Angels and archangels, I believe, are the Creator's messengers on Earth. They live on the spiritual plane but are assigned to look after human beings, hence the term 'guardian angel'. Our angels will help us to experience love in the most beautiful way. If you want your guardian angels to help you, then try the following ritual.

———— * ————

Asking Your Guardian Angels for Help

You will need:
* 5 green candles
* Photo of yourself during a very happy time

Take the candles, place them in a circle, then light them all. Green candles symbolise communication and the hope that your angels will use their celestial powers to heal you and bring happiness into your domain.

Place the photo in the middle of the circle.

Close your eyes and ask your angels to help you find love.

Once you have finished, open your eyes and thank your angels for their help.

I did this beautiful ritual around five years ago and I saw in my mind's eye a beautiful angel with huge golden wings. Its name was Seraphim. My guardian angel has helped me to develop the growing love I have for my two children. What is your guardian angel called? And what does it look like?

CONNECTING WITH YOUR GODDESS

Since time began different cultures have worshipped gods and goddesses. These deities were formed to help give people confidence and hope. All religions have their goddesses – you may be Catholic and believe in the Virgin Mary or Hindu and worship Shakti. Your goddess, whoever she is, can help you to tune in to the vibrations of love.

The fun part is choosing your own goddess of love. You can pick anyone, but here are a few examples for you to think about. You could also get a book containing the images of a range of goddesses. If you can get one, then sit quietly with the book in front of you and ask that your goddess be shown to you. Then close your eyes and choose a page. The one you pick is the goddess you should ask for help with your love life.

If you cannot get a book, here is a list of goddesses. Read the description of each and then choose the one that feels right for you.

Aphrodite She is the Greek goddess of love. She has the ability to bring soul mates together and she helps stabilise marriage. She can be contacted through burning frankincense incense and her symbol is the dolphin. The colour blue honours her.

Brighid She is the northern European goddess of women, love, healing and agriculture. If you want to honour her, use the colour white, especially white flowers.

Demeter She is the mother and the provider of fertile ground. She will bring with her a full and worthwhile relationship, one with few disappointments. Her sacred colour is purple and her symbol is the honeybee. She is queen of the harvest.

Freya She is the Norse goddess of love and marriage. She is the beginning, the middle and the end, and she is involved in all cycles. She brings with her fertility and happiness. Her symbol is the falcon and her colour is orange.

Venus She is the Roman goddess of love. She is an independent woman, but she does have time and space for love. The dove is her symbol and the apple is her fruit. The colour green is used in communicating with her.

———— * ————

Asking Your Goddess for Help

Choose which goddess you want to symbolise your future love.

Then take a candle in her colour and some objects to represent her symbols and make up an altar to her.

Light the candle and ask the goddess to help you in your

quest for love. Evoke her feminine power to grant your wishes.

By the time you have finished preparing yourself for love you will be looking and feeling great. All negativity will be banished. You will have put past hurts behind you and will have become more confident about yourself. You will have connected with your spiritual and emotional side and enlisted your helpers. Now we are going to see exactly how you can attract love into your life.

Chapter 2
HOW CAN YOU ATTRACT LOVE?

NOW YOU SHOULD BE emotionally and spiritually prepared to bring love into your life, we can move on to the very exciting stage which will see you learning ways to attract love. Again, there will be no psychobabble here, just honest advice using tried and tested rituals, personal development and plain old common sense.

YOUR PSYCHIC SPRING CLEAN

Before embarking on any important life-changing decisions it is essential to have a clean spirit and body. Since ancient times cleansing has been linked to many spiritual ceremonies, including those to do with the heart. My gran always used to wash her hands before doing any reading or healing. I would often ask her why and she would always reply, 'Clean spirit, clear spirit.' What she meant was that to be clean inside and out meant that the good things in life wouldn't pass you by.

Think about spring. It is a lovely image. It is the beginning of a new cycle when bulbs start to grow, lambs are born and there are the first signs that winter has finally gone for another year. It is the perfect time to cleanse and purify your body and soul. You don't have to wait until spring to do this, though – you can do it at any time of the year. Just let your imagination take you to springtime and the feelings that this would evoke. Imagine the sight of the yellow daffodils or the smell of the glorious hyacinths or the sound of birds nesting. I do this to prepare myself for readings and when I am opening mail from my readers.

You don't have to wait until spring to perform the following ritual either. Although it is termed 'psychic spring clean' it can be done all year round. I do it at least three times a year and the benefits are that I have a clear spirit, home and mind. It is also excellent in preparing you for love, as it clears away the emotional cobwebs that can gather around you. Emotional junk can cause you to feel low and tired and not the bright and breezy man-catcher you need to be.

———————— * ————————

Psychic Spring Clean

You will need:
* Sage smudge stick
* Some rose water
* Fresh pink rose petals
* Vacuum cleaner

* Natural duster or shammy leather
* Juice of 1 lemon
* Natural beeswax
* Distilled vinegar
* 2 bowls of water
* Newspaper or other paper
* Natural sponge or cotton flannel
* Natural soap
* Natural shampoo with rose extracts
* Pure geranium essential oil
* Pure rose essential oil

Give yourself time to carry out this ritual. It is not one to be rushed, so plan it carefully.

The first thing you must do is to clean your home from top to bottom. Vacuum up as much dust and dirt as possible. Then take a bowl of water and put the juice of 1 lemon in it. This serves as an excellent natural cleanser for all surfaces except for polished wood, which should be spruced up with natural beeswax. Make sure no surface is missed out. For windows, take the other bowl and pour 20 ml or 20 drops of distilled vinegar into about 250 ml (9 fl oz) of water. Use either newspaper or paper to clean up the windows. It's amazing how effective this is. It's a tip from my mum, whose windows always sparkle. Then use the natural cloth or leather shammy to dust all your surfaces.

Having cleaned your whole house (I told you it would take time, didn't I?), you now need to clean yourself, body and mind.

How Can You Attract Love?

Run a bath for yourself and add 4 drops of rose oil and 4 drops of geranium oil to it. These oils will help you relax and keep you balanced. The rose is also linked to the heart chakra and helps to open it up to the possibility of love. Geranium is a hormonal balancer and helps to calm your emotions. Then add real pink rose petals. I know they're a luxury, but you're worth it. Then get in, lie back and relax.

Close your eyes and imagine you are on top of a hill looking out onto the most beautiful natural landscape. You can see green fields, luscious valleys and young rivers. From your viewpoint the world is a beautiful spiritual place. The air is fresh and clean. You can smell the grass, flowers and trees. Then slowly open your eyes and feel at peace and happy. Your mind is now cleansed and your body is next.

To cleanse your body, wash using a natural sponge or cotton flannel and natural soap – you know, the yummy kinds you can get at shops such as Lush or The Body Shop. Wash your hair using a natural shampoo, preferably with rose extracts. Rose is used throughout this ritual as it represents pure and gentle love. You are clearing the way for this kind of love to enter your life.

Now get dressed in clean fresh clothes in either pink or red, depending on your preference, and thank your Higher Self for cleansing you.

Then go around every corner of your house with the smudge stick and let its smoke and aroma clear all negativity from your house. Pay particular attention to the corners, as stagnant energy can build up there. A smudge stick is normally made up of sage leaves bound with twine.

It was used by the Native Americans to banish bad spirits or negative energy from their living spaces. I use it all the time, in spite of my husband's moaning, as he hates the smell. But it works.

Sprinkle some rose water at your front door or the main door to your house. This is a sign that this house is now ready to let love enter it.

Sit in your favourite room and imagine that your house is filled with brilliant violet light which is coming from the Moon above. This will cleanse your house using colour.

Finally, take time for quiet reflection and say a prayer in honour of your home and its living spirit.

———— * ————

You and your home are now psychically cleansed and ready for the new future which awaits you.

WHO IS RIGHT FOR YOU?

I believe that there is a soul out there for all of us. Just as there is Yin and Yang and strawberries and cream, so there is you and a soul mate. But just who is it? Here I want to explore proven ways of finding out.

DREAM HIM ...

In order to recognise someone who will be a compatible partner for you, you need to focus on what your needs and dreams are. You can't expect a lover to appear if you don't know who or what you like. And you can't begin to make a relationship happy until you are happy yourself. So unlock your dreams and unlock the possibility of meeting your dream lover.

As you begin to become aware of your psychic ability and intuitive side you will find that you dream more. So keep a notebook at the side of your bed. Before you go to sleep at night think about the type of person you would like to spend the rest of your life with. What sort of personality would they have? What would they look like? Do you know them already? Think about it and take the time to make notes. If you have a mental image of who they are, then it is easier to know what you are looking for.

In a matter of weeks you may find yourself dreaming of this person. Each time you wake, use your notebook to jot down all the details of the dream. Colours, smells, location and events will all mean something and give you clues as to who your dream partner will be.

I did this myself as a teenager and dreamt of a Greek god with curly hair playing a harp for me. Two years later I met Ronald and one of the things which struck me about him was his curly hair. I bet you're wondering where the harp came into it? Well, he played the guitar and wrote me songs. Weird, I know, but completely true.

———————*———————

Dream Lover Meditation

Meditation is an amazing tool for clearing your mind of all the problems you have to deal with on a day-to-day basis. Slowing your mind will allow you to listen to a most prized possession: *your inner voice*. This will reflect your heart's desires and allow you to express them more easily.

Meditation will also relax your body and mind so that when you sleep you have a better chance of dreaming. I meditate as often as I can before I go to sleep. Sleep is my favourite hobby and meditation allows me to have a peaceful night's sleep, which is a great bonus. Of course you can do this meditation at any time of the day or night; I just prefer to do it before I sleep.

For this meditation you will need to sit on the floor so that you connect with the Earth and are grounded. Being grounded simply means that you are solidly anchored in the present. You feel secure and are in control of yourself. If I am not grounded I feel anxious and unfocused and can't concentrate. I am sure you will have felt like that from time to time.

I normally do this meditation on a big cosy cover which I place on the floor of my bedroom. You can use a cushion or duvet, whatever makes you feel warm and secure, like a security blanket I suppose.

Sit cross-legged as best you can, as none of us are getting any younger. If you are unable to sit on the floor for any reason then you can just sit on a chair with a cover over you. Make sure your back is straight. This also means that you are breathing properly. Gently clasp your hands in front of you. Then close your eyes.

As thoughts come into your head, let them enter then let them leave again. Empty your thoughts one by one – don't hold on to any worries, problems or ideas.

To make it easier for myself, I imagine a large Welsh dresser with crockery on top and shelves and a drawer and cupboard below. It is made of antique pine and I can smell the wood. As each worry or thought enters my mind I just put it in the drawer to be dealt with another time. Soon my head is clear of all the junk that has been swirling about it all day.

Now, having cleared your mind, focus on your breathing. Take a deep breath in, slowly counting to five as you do so. Then breathe out slowly, again over a count of five. Listen to your breath and feel it. This is the very force which keeps you alive.

Now breathe in and out five times and just concentrate on your breathing. Focus on the here and now, your breath and the miracle of it. You will now feel relaxed and in control.

Do this for about 10 minutes, then slowly come back to your surroundings. Open your eyes. Be aware of the room around you – what it looks like, how it smells and where you are in it. Having come to your senses you will feel good and relaxed.

This meditation should be done a couple of times a week. I know how busy life is, but this really will help you to cope better. It will also train your mind to look for information you normally wouldn't even notice. This information could be vitally important in recognising your soul mate. You will learn to pick up on the slightest of signs from people you meet and these could all lead to your dream man.

I had a colleague at a magazine I once worked for who was single and very scatty. She would forget the most mundane things, such as the lunch she had made that morning or the fact that she had a dental appointment that day. Her head was all over the place and so she would never pick up on the signals men gave her. I gave her a copy of this meditation and within six weeks both she and her colleagues had noticed a difference. She was more grounded and saw for the first time that the picture editor fancied her. This meditation will help you see more clearly too.

NUMEROLOGY AND ROMANCE

Pythagoras first devised numerology in 600 BC. It is a system in which numbers relate to people's everyday lives.

I personally am a great believer in the power of numbers in our lives. My favourite number is eight and it is no surprise to me that this is seen as an infinite number with no beginning or end. It is also the number of the mystic and it has governed my life for many years. For example, my house number is 116, which added together to a single digit makes eight. I was born in August, the eighth month; I was also married in that month.

Numbers do dominate our lives, so it is not surprising that they can dominate our relationships too. Numerology has the power to reveal the influence our names and dates of birth have on our lives. The very essence of your name and the sound it makes connect you to your identity. Numerology also brings rhythm to our lives, as numbers follow cyclical patterns.

To know who you are compatible with you need to know your 'personality number'. This gives information about your psychological make-up, your relationships and your outlook on life. It is therefore a great way of seeing what other personality types you would be compatible with. The rule of thumb is that you use the name you were born with, the one on your birth certificate. This is the core of your personality. It is who you are. I am afraid that shortened names or nicknames will not work in this case. Middle names should be used also, if they are on the birth certificate.

How to Discover Your Personality Number

Although I did a science degree, maths was never my strong point, but I am glad to say that numerology calculations are very simple, so don't be put off!

Just take the number of each letter of your name, according to the table on page 62, and add them together until you get a number below 10. Follow the instructions below the table to ascertain how well suited you are to a potential partner.

Using John Smith as an example:

John = 1 + 6 + 8 + 5

Add the numbers together: 1 + 6 + 8 + 5 = 20

Now add 2 + 0 together so that the number is below 10: 2 + 0 = 2

Now do the same again for Smith.

Smith = 1 + 4 + 9 + 2 + 8

Add all the numbers together: 1 + 4 + 9 + 2 + 8 = 24

2 + 4 = 6

Finally add the two numbers from the two names: 2 + 6 = 8

John Smith's personality number is 8.

NUMBER COMPATABILITIES

HER PN \ HIS PN	1	2	3	4
1	You will have a sporty high-octane life. Energetic mix.	A loving match, as you understand one another.	You will go into orbit with this match.	Sensuous, sexy mix; lots of sexy fun.
2	Sensitive 2 will enjoy the varoom 1 gives.	You will both want to cuddle up and stay at home.	You will both travel and seek new experiences.	Physical attraction will make way to physical relation.
3	You will find this person mentally stimulating.	A 2 will welcome you home from work.	Your perfect soulmate – you both live life to the full.	You will be best as partners in business.
4	Great match filled with fun and laughter.	What language do they speak? It isn't yours.	You will both live life to the full.	You will find this person too similar to make it work.
5	Mentally this person can't stimulate you enough.	You will feel loved and cherished.	You won't be able to control a 3.	Your 4 will keep you mentally stimulated.
6	A romantic mix – it will be great.	A great relationship with positive outcomes.	Not refined enough for you.	Communication would be a problem.
7	Not the best match as the 1 can sometimes smother you.	An initial attraction may end in you being let down.	Sensual mix of business and pleasure.	You will never be bored with this mix.
8	You have no way of controlling this person.	Well suited as you both have similar goals.	Has a chance to flourish if you learn to accept men.	Great relationship in the long term.
9	Exciting match.	Share same spiritual ideals.	A lively mix.	This person would bore the pants off you.

How Can You Attract Love?

5	6	7	8	9
Intense and can cause arguments.	You will be good friends but not much else.	They will tend to wander so trust is a big issue here.	Big power fights over who is in control.	An interest is there but needs to be nurtured.
You both want different things so hard to make a couple.	You love the 6's beauty – it reflects good on you.	A 7 could limit your dreams and aspirations.	The number 8 will bring out the worst in you, so not great.	This number will love you and protect you.
A 5 will never bore you and travel big on agenda.	A busy relationship with many aspects.	In a marriage you will never be bored.	They may find your wanderlust too much.	Very creative relationship.
You can't keep up with them so may give up.	A great aspect – solid as a rock.	They don't make you feel secure enough.	You will have great finances and wealth.	Very highly charged and emotional.
You love to talk the same language.	Possibilities endless as you have wanderlust personified.	Their body language will not be right for you.	Both tend to focus on the same goals.	A great friendship which can develop.
May find that you both don't have the same outlook.	You both will fight for the mirror.	You are both on the same wavelength.	Very passionate union.	Sensual and also intelligent mix.
Travel, and a dream to be successful, will keep love.	This person's grooming could in the end be their downfall.	You are both coming from the same place.	Your approach is too practical for an 8.	Heaven-made relationship.
A 5 is too much of an airhead for you.	Sensual sexual highs.	Irritates you as too head in the clouds.	Good positive outcome here.	Too many silly arguments to make it work.
Travel through life aiming for the same things.	Passionate mix.	Communication not quite right.	Too cautious and prim for your needs.	Too samey; minus no challenge.

NUMERICAL VALUES								
1	2	3	4	5	6	7	8	9
A	B	C	D	E	F	G	H	I
J	K	L	M	N	O	P	Q	R
S	T	U	V	W	X	Y	Z	

Now that you know your personality number you can use the tables on pages 60–62 to see which numbers are compatible with you. When you meet someone you will be able to check out whether you are well suited numerologically or if the numbers just don't add up. This is all great fun – don't take it too seriously. It is just another string to your bow.

ASTROLOGICAL COMPATIBILITY

Astrologers believe that the arrangement of the planets in the sky at birth forms your personality. The arrangement is shown on a birth chart, which gives great insights into your character and how you will interact with other people. As a guide to compatibility, it is a great and fun tool.

I am a typical Leo. I am outgoing yet sensitive and very, very loyal. My husband, on the other hand, is an Aries. He is sporty and thinks he is always right. When we met the first thing I checked was the compatibility chart my grannie gave me and which I am passing on to you now (*see pages 64–69*). Seemingly we are the most perfect match of the zodiac and after 14 years of marriage I am beginning to think that's true.

How Can You Attract Love?

Have a look at your star sign and see which ones you are compatible with. It will give you an idea, but remember this is not an exact science and is for guidance only.

The 12 star signs can be divided into four elements which characterise those born under each Sun sign:

Fire Aries, Leo, Sagittarius.
In love these signs are volatile, energetic and uninhibited. They are lovable, loyal and enjoy a varied sexual appetite.

Earth Taurus, Virgo, Capricorn
Practical and cautious in love. They take time to trust a lover, but once they do they are loyal and loving.

Air Gemini, Libra, Aquarius
Dreamers who love love and many find their dreams unrealised, but when they fall in love they are very romantic.

Water Cancer, Scorpio, Pisces
Very emotional and intuitive, they will never hide how they feel. What you see is what you get.

The charts on pages 64–69 show astrological compatibilities. The key below gives you a general idea of what the symbols mean.

☺ Same wavelength – will make great friends and lovers with time.

☹ No chemistry and will find each other a turn off.

☺☺ A lot of tension so fighting and arguments likely.

♡ Love and passion – the perfect match.

ϟϟϟ You will love each other but also drive each other mad!

ASTROLOGICAL COMPATIBILITIES
GIRLS

	Capricorn	Aquarius	Pisces	Aries
Capricorn	Careers come first.	Nothing to talk about.	Good balance.	Not in this lifetime.
Aquarius	No chemistry.	Short relationship.	He will bore you.	Same sense of humour.
Pisces	Special love.	Don't waste your time.	Opposites do attract.	Touchy with no feeling.
Aries	Opposites.	Happy pair of nuts.	Arguments weekly.	Never a dull moment.
Taurus	A great match.	Too many arguments.	Love will blossom.	Unequal backgrounds.
Gemini	Big problems.	Different but there's attraction.	Worlds collide.	Romance will last.

GUYS

ASTROLOGICAL COMPATIBILITIES
GIRLS

	Capricorn	Aquarius	Pisces	Aries
Cancer	⚡⚡⚡ No way.	🙁 Too sensitive.	🖤 One in a million love.	😶💫😶 His way or the highway.
Leo	🙁 Both career people.	⚡⚡⚡ Love and war.	🙁 Not a success.	🖤 Hot all over the place.
Virgo	🖤 Yippee.	🙁 Her head is in the clouds.	⚡⚡⚡ Fighting friends.	🙁 Lifestyles differ.
Libra	😶💫😶 Financially unequal.	🖤 Love.	🙁 Not suitable.	⚡⚡⚡ Kiss then miss.
Scorpio	🙂 Strong bond.	😶💫😶 Too stubborn.	🖤 Hot as chilli.	🙁 Poles collide.
Sagittarius	🙁 Highly unlikely.	🙂 Mates and lovers.	😶💫😶 It's war.	🖤 What a carry on.

GUYS

ASTROLOGICAL COMPATIBILITIES
GIRLS

	Taurus	Gemini	Cancer	Leo
Capricorn	Meeting in heaven.	Poles apart.	Mood swings.	Lack of communication.
Aquarius	Too similar.	Great match.	No common ground.	Love/hate relationship.
Pisces	Some likes and dislikes.	Good sparring partners.	Hot, hot, hot.	No challenge, no hope.
Aries	Money will be an issue.	Long walks, long love life.	Family will cause friction.	Chilli hot.
Taurus	Passionate fights.	Can't trust him/her.	Safe and sound.	Poles apart.
Gemini	She is too sporty.	Like twins.	Too close to her family.	Great social couple.

GUYS

ASTROLOGICAL COMPATIBILITIES
GIRLS

	Taurus	Gemini	Cancer	Leo
Cancer	Great together.	He's a mummy's boy.	You go one way, he goes another.	She will overpower you.
Leo	Boxing gloves on.	Party people.	She needs her mum too much.	Battle of the egos.
Virgo	Very experimental.	Don't even go there.	True friends and partners.	Not compatible.
Libra	Needs not matched.	Friends and lovers.	War of words.	Friends first then lovers.
Scorpio	Passion then argue.	Silent treatment.	Match made in heaven.	No go.
Sagittarius	Too stressful.	Bing, bang, wham.	Too big a challenge.	Romance and fun.

GUYS

ASTROLOGICAL COMPATIBILITIES
GIRLS

	Virgo	Libra	Scorpio	Sagittarius
Capricorn	Come from same background.	Too similar.	Happy times.	Nothing in common.
Aquarius	Frustrating union.	A perfect 10.	Don't see eye to eye.	Share wanderlust.
Pisces	Perfectly imperfect.	Too many differences.	Meeting of minds.	It will end very quickly.
Aries	Too alike.	You will love to hate.	No, just won't work.	Laugh a minute.
Taurus	Fruitful union.	Different views.	Attraction but fatal.	Yes it's love.
Gemini	She will nag you, he will too.	Great communication.	Shady past.	Can't bridge the gap.

GUYS

ASTROLOGICAL COMPATIBILITIES
GIRLS

	Virgo	Libra	Scorpio	Sagittarius
Cancer	Both love children.	Argue at the drop of a hat.	Passion wagon.	Starts off OK then goes downhill.
Leo	Too picky for him.	Thumbs up.	Slanging matches.	Well matched.
Virgo	Too anal together.	Keeping secrets.	Steady relationship.	Arguments all day long.
Libra	He tells porkies.	No X factor.	Not matched.	Everyday happy.
Scorpio	Best pals.	Can't work.	Too high octane.	Match made in hell.
Sagittarius	Fists and raised voices.	Great couple.	Too unhappy.	Lust.

GUYS

MAGIC HIM UP!

You can also use rituals and the magic of nature to bring your mate to you. All magic is used to create harmony and bring balance to a situation. Be careful what you wish for and make sure you never use magic to make someone do something against their will. Never hurt someone with it, as it will only come back to haunt you. You will need to believe in what you are doing, so a positive attitude will help. Also, you can't force someone to love you – they must decide of their own free will. Ask for someone who will be good for you, as you might have an idea in mind but the universe could give you someone far better.

Magic Mr Right

You will need:
* 2 small magnets
* Musk oil
* Amber incense
* 2 pictures or small statues to represent a man and a woman
* 2 red candles
* White paper
* Red pen

Find a quiet place in the house where you can build a love altar. It can be anywhere – a windowsill, or on top of a CD rack, like mine – as long as it is safe and won't be disturbed. A flat surface is best, so have a look around your house just now and find the perfect spot.

Put the two red candles at either side of the altar for love and passion. Then place the figure representing you and the one representing your future man at either end of the altar. The magnets will attract love to you – place one by each figure.

Anoint the candles by gently rubbing them with the musk oil. Light them and then use them to light the amber incense, leaving it in the middle of the altar. Your incense will purify the altar and help love to surface.

Next comes the very important bit. Sit down quietly and just think about your intentions. What do you really want out of this? *Who* do you want out of this? Look at the flame of the red candles and then write down what you want out of a relationship. The red ink on the white paper will seal the magic and love will come into your life.

Once you have done this, take the piece of paper and fold it into a small square. Put it in the centre of the altar and then close your eyes and thank your spirit guides and Higher Self for helping you.

Now you are free to go about your normal business.

———*———

I would do this ritual once every two weeks until you meet your lover.

FOLLOW YOUR INTUITION

Opening up your intuition will mean you will not let Mr Right pass you by. Don't allow this to happen – he is out there. You may see him at any time – in a park, at work or when you are out for the night. Awaken your psychic senses now.

The next ritual will stimulate your psychic powers and activate your intuition so that the man of your dreams will not be overlooked. Could you imagine how awful it would be for that to happen? Do the following simple ritual to ensure you recognise every opportunity Fate deals you. In it you will call upon the power and insight of Neptune, god of the sea and planet of visions and fantasy.

————————*————————

Sea Ritual to See Clearly

You will need:
* Something to represent Neptune as god of the sea – a statue or a picture will do
* A couple of seashells
* Water in a bowl, preferably one of clear glass
* Piece of cloth coloured sea-blue
* Love heart symbol – a charm or picture will suffice
* Sea-blue candle

Make sure you are able to spend time and energy on this ritual and that you are away from any distractions such as children or pets. The ritual can be done at any time of the day or night just as long as you don't rush it.

Find a table or another flat surface to do your ritual on and then place the blue cloth on it. Take your picture or repre-sentation of Neptune and place it in the middle of the table. Then put your seashells either side of it. Your water bowl should then be set down facing Neptune. Place the love heart symbol in the water. Finally, light your candle.

How Can You Attract Love?

Sit quietly and listen to your breathing. Breathe slowly and close your eyes. Focus on the sea and think about its power. Imagine you can see right to the very bottom of the sea. You can glimpse the sea bed and above it the fish and other sea creatures swimming about. You feel pleased that the sea is such a magical place.

Now slowly take your mind away from the sea and bring it back to your room. Imagine a purple beam of light coming from the skies above and entering your third eye. This is found in the middle of your forehead. It is also known as the sixth chakra and is the centre of your inner sight, your mind's eye. Now concentrate on your breathing again.

Slowly open your eyes. You will feel refreshed. Thank Neptune for his help in giving you the ability to see visions and use your psychic senses.

In this ritual the blue cloth and candle represent healing, which you will go through as you find love. The water is the sea and the heart placed in it represents the visions that will now be unlocked. Neptune, as I mentioned, is the visionary planet as well as god of the sea and that is why he is great for this purpose.

After you have done this ritual you may discover that your psychic senses will be open in all aspects of your life, not just love. When you meet a new man you may find that you get a really strong positive vibe. This is telling you that he is special, so you need to get to know him a whole lot better. Or you may find that you get dreams which show you who your lover will be. Make a note of them in your dream journal. Write down all the information you can, as it will come in handy.

You have great tools in place now which will be useful as you start looking for love.

WHERE TO FIND LOVE

By now you have had your spring clean, you should have a good idea of the type of person you are compatible with and your psychic senses have been tuned in, so you are ready to find your soul mate. The next big question is: where to look?

So many people write to me saying they can't find love. Then when you look more deeply, you discover that they never go anywhere where they might meet a suitable partner. If you want to find love, then you must make an effort to go out and look for it. It won't come looking for you.

Before you embark on your quest to find a partner, though, try this ritual. It will set the wheels in motion and prepare you for love.

———————*———————

Finding a New Lover

You will need:
* 6 pink candles
* Piece of rose quartz
* Fresh basil
* Ceramic/earthenware bowl

Do this ritual during the waxing phase of the Moon on a Friday night. Friday is the day for empowering love rituals and the waxing phase of the Moon helps to draw love to you. (The waxing phase is when the Moon is growing in size to a Full Moon.)

Take the candles and place them in a circle on your love altar, the one you prepared during the 'Magic Mr Right' ritual (*see pages 70–71*). There are six candles as six is the number representing love in numerology. This is very powerful symbolism in this ritual and it works. Then place the rose quartz in the middle of the circle. The basil should be in the bowl and placed outside the circle.

Once everything is on your altar, light your candles. Pick up the bowl with the basil (basil draws love) and say:

> *'I am ready for love. Basil, draw it to me.*
> *I am ready for love. Let it find me.'*

Then close your eyes and thank all the positive forces of nature for helping you to find your special person.

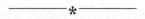

I have a friend in Turkey who tried this ritual for me, as it has elements of Turkish and Romany magic in it. She met a suitable husband a month later at a fish restaurant when sharing a meal with her family. So the magic you make here can work all over the world.

TRADITIONAL PLACES TO FIND LOVE

Chances are that you will meet someone when you least expect it. This can happen anywhere, but getting out socially will increase your opportunities. Clubs, pubs and wine bars, classes and societies, sports clubs and events and holidays are all potential hotspots for your love interest.

Clubs, Pubs and Wine Bars

Clubs are great places to see what the opposite sex has to offer and are full of singles dressed to kill and on the pull. They are not always the best way to find a meaningful relationship, but they can bring results. And that is what this book is all about!

A great way to prepare for a night out is to do what I call 'a Friday night spell'. Be sure to do it on a Friday night.

A Friday Night Spell

There are no candles involved in this and it is so simple. Place the clothes you will be wearing on your bed and spray them with your favourite perfume. As you do this say three times:

'*Scent of mine, make a good-looking man be mine.*'

Your clothes will now be charged up just like a love magnet, so that eligible men won't be able to resist you.

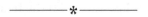

When you are in pubs or wine bars with friends, you will not only be able to eye up the talent but also, if need be, to get yourself noticed through exuding confidence and a positive body image. You will have both by now! Always remember to be well groomed, attractively dressed and have your mind magnet on (*see pages 30–31*). Wearing hot pink will attract the sweetest love to you. If you want raunchy sex, then wear red. These colours will activate your chakras as nothing else can.

Classes and Societies

One of the pieces of advice I normally give to people who are searching for love is to go to night classes. This is for three reasons: they will learn a new skill, they will meet new people and they will gain in confidence. At a class you will also get the chance to meet people who are on the same wavelength as you are, which from a psychic perspective is always a great start.

Societies, perhaps public speaking or local history ones, are another great way to meet new people. They can be fun too, which is important. The possibilities are endless and you are in control, you can make it happen.

The best place to find out about classes and clubs is your local library or community centre. The Internet is also a brilliant way of discovering what is going on in your area.

Local schools and colleges usually hold a variety of classes, from Latin American dancing to pottery. Have a look and expand your horizons. A client of mine met her husband at a salsa class – and what a way to meet someone. Barriers are down right away when you need to dance with someone, especially when learning a seductive dance like a tango. You get to hold them close – and all in the name of learning!

Classes and societies will also develop you as a person and this in turn will increase your potential. When Mr Right does come along he is not going to pass Miss Potential by!

Sports Clubs

In the past three years I have noticed an increase in the number of people writing to me who have found a partner at a gym. It is a double whammy going to a health or sports club as you will get fit as well as meet eligible people. So get out and join your gym or local judo club – Mr Right could be just a skip away!

Work

Have you ever thought that your work is a possible place to find love? Instead of being the daily grind it could be just the opportunity you have been waiting for.

I had a lady come to me for a reading a couple of years ago. She was looking for love and I kept seeing a lift as being significant. I knew her work was also involved but didn't know how or when. Six months later she e-mailed me to let me know that a guy she saw every day in a lift going to work had finally asked her out. Sometimes what I see seems crazy, but it eventually makes sense. So my advice is to open your eyes to every opportunity.

At work you should make sure that you have the scent of rose and musk around you. Of course it is not easy to light candles or burn incense at work, but you could have a bowl with pot pourri in it. The scent of rose will awaken the senses of those around you to love and musk is an aroma that attracts men to women, as it is similar to female pheromones. Pheromones are the smells the sexes give off to attract each other. Another great tip is to wear red or pink for love, or blue if you want to increase communication with a colleague you fancy.

Holidays

I could write a book on holiday romances. I have had literally hundreds of letters this year alone from people who have met a special someone on holiday. They normally write begging me to say that I see it lasting forever. Normally when I do the reading for them my bones have other ideas altogether . . .

Holiday romances often work out initially because on holiday you are relaxed and have your guard down, which makes it easier for love to blossom. However, the downside is that the relationship is unreal and when you come back home and back down to Earth the dream can be shattered.

Having said that, I do know of holiday romances that have lasted. It just depends on the factors at work such as distance, willingness to work really hard at the relationship and finally whether you still fancy your holiday lover in the cold light of day. As usual my motto here is 'Be careful and never jeopardise your safety.' Holidays can bring true romance, though, so don't knock them until you have tried one. If you want to know if your holiday romance is really the one, try the following ritual.

—————*—————

Holiday Romance Ritual

You will need:
* Silver-coloured bowl
* White candle

Take the bowl and half fill it with water.

Then take the white candle, for truth, and light it. As it

burns, ask your guides to reveal to you whether your holiday romance is real or a passing phase.

Then allow the wax to fall into the water six times, the number associated with love.

Extinguish the candle and take a look in the bowl. The six pieces of wax will have made shapes. If any look like an animal or insect, then the answer to your question is 'yes'. If not, then the answer is 'no'.

Friends

Each and every one of your friends is an amazing source of meeting a whole lot of other people. Dinner parties, parties and any other gatherings of friends are ideal events at which to meet a potential partner. Furthermore, your friends know you and will be able to put you in touch with people they deem suitable for you.

Why not get your friends to organise a few events and just enjoy what materialises in front of you? Remember to connect with your spirit guides or guardian angels as well. They will help you, so try to sense the subtle messages they give you. For example, a friend of mine who worked as a teacher in, of all places, LA, told me that during a dinner party she kept sensing that someone was standing behind her. Every time she looked around no one was there. Finally she turned around and almost fell into the arms of a guy who had been trying to attract her attention all night. She was sure it was her guardian angel making sure she didn't miss him and they are now living happily ever after.

Your angels are nearby, so just tune in to their signals as you did before (*see pages 46–47*).

Dating Agencies

I know lots of people who are single but who wouldn't touch a dating agency with a barge pole. This is unfortunate, as they are great ways to be introduced to people who are likely to share the same interests as you. Apart from that, you can normally control whom you meet and are able to choose your dates from a safe stress-free distance.

If you decide that a dating agency is the way to progress in your love search, then make sure that the company you choose is a reputable one which checks the details of all their clients carefully. You don't want to end up with an axe murderer!

Before choosing a date, just sit quietly and relax. That way you will be able to make your decision more clearly.

A client once asked me if I could possibly take a look at the particulars of five guys she had been given information about. She had spent £750 on membership of an exclusive dating agency. I sat and looked at all their photographs, and number 1142, which is all I knew about him at that point, seemed to me the obvious choice. I just felt he was the one. She trusted my instincts and married number 1142, who turned out to be an airline pilot.

As I won't be around to choose Mr Right for you personally, I would suggest you get yourself a pendulum. They are available in any good New Age or magic shop or can be bought by mail order. Even a necklace with a ring on it will do. You can use your pendulum to dowse, which is a method of answering specific questions. You are getting the answers from the universe and your inner self.

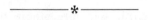

Dowsing

Make sure you have peace and quiet to do your dowsing. You want your senses to take you in the right direction and that can only happen if you are at peace.

Sit comfortably and hold the pendulum with your right hand. You first need to find out what is 'yes' and 'no'. So ask it a question which has a negative answer such as 'Have I got 10 children?' Note how it swings. It will do so of its own accord. Then try a question you know has a positive answer. You now know what is 'yes' and 'no'.

To get into the 'love groove', think about how you feel when you are in love. Then, if you have a list of possible dates you want to check out, go through it asking whether you should choose each person. Once you have finished, thank the universe for its help and get your date sorted out. That person could be the one you have been looking for.

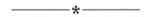

I know dating agencies are not everyone's cup of tea, but they can still bring results.

Lonely Hearts Ads

Aaaaah, the personal columns of any paper used to bring me hours of amusement. 'Tall businessman looking for blonde bombshell . . .' Joking aside, over the past 10 years they have become sophisticated. Now in many cases you can hear a prerecorded message of the person then choose to leave a reply and set up a date. A very good friend of mine met someone this way and he turned out to be a real catch.

To ensure the best results, use the pendulum as I explained earlier, only this time dowsing over the newspaper column and asking about all the ads you are interested in. Try questions like 'Are you looking for a long-term thing?' or even 'Are you always faithful in a relationship?'

If you do meet someone, you must make sure that it is in a safe, well-populated place and that someone knows where you will be. You should also protect yourself psychically. A great way to do this is the following.

———— * ————

Psychic Protection

Sit comfortably with your body relaxed, eyes closed and mind still.

Now imagine that you have a torch just above the top of your head. It is pointing downwards and is switched off just now.

Imagine that you have pressed the switch to turn it on and its beam of light is shining down on you. Allow this bright white light to cover your whole body, offering you spiritual, emotional and physical protection from all beings and elements.

You can now look at eligible dates with the added comfort of psychic protection.

———————*———————

FINDING LOVE IN THE 21st CENTURY

Nowadays finding love has become a multimillion-pound business and it's changing all the time. New ideas and technology have been developed which will become the dating agencies and lonely hearts columns of the not-too-distant future. As I write, many of these innovative new ways to connect with people are here already and they make the future of dating very exciting indeed. I am looking at four examples here and they are the Internet, computer dating, speed dating and shag tags. I will explain all in a minute, especially the last one, and yes, the mind boggles.

Love in the 21st century is all about finding a quality mate who can give you what you want while you are still able to work and develop your career and interests. I know that sounds cold, but to find love at times takes precision and a keen business sense. Romance does follow, but you have to locate your prince first.

The Internet

If anyone had told us 20 years ago that we would be able to get in touch with millions of people at the touch of a button we would have probably thought that they were crazy. But it's true and what an amazing thing the Internet is. I would be lost without it.

Over the past two years I've been contacted at least 100 times by people asking me for advice on their cyber-relationships – relationships with someone they have fallen in love with in an Internet chat room but usually haven't ever set eyes on. Chat rooms are certainly a great way of meeting people. The problem comes from the fact that in many cases you only have the person's word for who and what they are. You normally can't see them and therefore trust plays an important part in the relationship. Chat rooms are good, however, in that you are able to hook up with people who like the same things as you do. I must admit I have never been in a chat room, but from what I hear it can get incredibly intimate.

Again, the most important factor is safety. Try to be aware of exactly what you are getting involved in. I had a woman write to me only a short time ago. She was willing to give up her marriage and her children to move to Texas to be with a guy she had only ever communicated with over the Internet. I was so glad to warn her against doing this as I could clearly see that this man had been lying to her. He was married and had children all over the place, not just with his wife.

Not everyone is lucky enough to have me around to check things out, so you need to use your intuition as well as the Internet. Does your gut feeling tell you that the person you are chatting to is being honest? A good tip is to have a blue candle burning near the computer, as blue is a colour which will help you seek the truth. Also burning basil essential oil will keep you alert so that you can pick up all signals coming from the other person through their e-mail.

Computer Dating

Many Internet providers will be able to supply you with computer-dating sites. You just need to have the incentive to go out and look for them. They are just like the lonely hearts columns you would get in a newspaper, only you find them on the net.

People can't be closely vetted in these, so again be careful about what information you give out and if you plan to follow up a contact then be sure you are safe. Computer dating could be music to your ears, though, so don't rule it out. I do know a very choosy career girl in her thirties who after five years of trying to find Mr Right was introduced to him via a computer-dating business. She felt that the choices she had on the site she looked at were endless and choosing her perfect partner was the icing on the cake. She is now happily married.

If you do decide to use computer dating, you might like to try the following.

———————*———————

Choosing Computer Dates

You will need:
* Some pink paper or card
* Pair of scissors
* Bowl

Write out a list of possible dates on the pink paper or card, giving each one a number. Then take a pair of scissors and cut out each one. Fold them up, then put them all into a bowl and ask your spirit guides to help you choose the dates most suited to you.

Then close your eyes and place your left hand in the bowl. You should feel guided to choose as many as your guides see fit. Then open your eyes and see which date you have chosen.

As usual, remember to thank your guides for their assistance.

Speed Dating

As far as I know this hasn't really caught on this side of the pond yet. But in Seattle there are seven men to one woman, so speed dating has been devised as a quick way to meet a great many women in a short space of time. Seattle is a place where career tends to come first, but the men are finding that they are missing out on love – well, that is what I heard on an edition of *Oprah* a couple of months back.

With speed dating, what you do is have seven dates in one night. They normally all take place in a coffee bar or wine bar and each person is allocated a set time for each date, for example five minutes. And at the end of meeting your seven candidates you get to choose whether any are your cup of tea.

If you are a business type with little social time to spare, then speed dating could be for you. I even saw it on an episode of *Sabrina the Teenage Witch* recently. You never know, it might eventually catch on in Britain. If you ever get the chance to do speed dating I would suggest you try to keep calm and use each introduction as a social rather than romantic meeting. Then you won't feel under so much pressure and will enjoy the experience. Calm mind equals calm aura and allows you to pick up on possible signals which could lead to romance.

Shag Tags

Quite a coarse name you may think, but bars, clubs and pubs in Glasgow, Manchester and to a lesser degree London have been having 'shag tag nights'.

What you do is take a tag and put a number on it, then wear it in a prominent position on your person. Then when you see someone you like, you check their number and write it up on a board which is displayed in a prominent place, often the bar. You put your number next to their number and when they see that you can meet up. This way there is no beating about the bush – they know you fancy them. Of course there is the chance that you may be rejected or, if you are chosen, that you don't fancy the other person. That is the thrill of the game – you make your bets and take your chances. It is great fun, but certainly for younger people, I guess. What would I know – I am in my thirties, for goodness' sake!

If you ever get the chance to play a game of shag tags, make sure you wear something purple, as this colour will only draw people who are on your wavelength. Try to choose someone with good vibes, as this is an indication that they will be suitable for you. If you feel good vibes, then that is your intuition telling you that person is a distinct possibility.

MAKING YOUR MOVE

So what do you do if you do see a guy you really fancy? It's no use letting him pass you by. Just go over and introduce yourself ... or become a love goddess who can flirt outrageously. Just follow my tips and you will be successful.

I know this sounds scary, but remember the rituals I have shown you for becoming powerful and positive? Also, recall that friends are great and they can help introduce you to the guy you fancy. You never know, they might even know him, which is even better.

If you have to introduce yourself, don't panic, just remember the three most important things:

1. Smile.

2. Make eye contact.

3. Have a pen and paper ready to leave a contact number.

Smile If you smile and he smiles back then you know that it is a good time to introduce yourself. Once you do, keep on smiling, as it shows that you are having a good time and that you like what you see. A smile will spread loving vibrations between the two of you. And pink lipstick will reveal that you are out to find love.

Make eye contact The eyes are the windows of the soul and making eye contact is sure to get his attention. If he holds your gaze for at least four seconds across a room, you will know that he's interested. If he keeps looking around, then you are in. When you finally meet, keep your glances short, as this will give you both time to feel comfortable in each other's company. Looking at a man also gives you the chance to size him up. Your intuition will be activated, so go with what it is telling you. If you feel warmth when you are looking into his eyes then he is likely to be compatible with you. If, however, you feel uneasy, then he will not be for you. Listen to your intuition.

Leave a contact number You don't want to lose touch, so have pen and paper with you or if possible a card with your name and contact number on it. It helps if you have placed the pen and paper on the altar we spoke of earlier with the red candles (*see page 75*). This will energise them in your love quest. Remember, only give out details that you are happy with, such as mobile phone number. Don't give out your address until you know the person better.

Doing these three things will mean that you won't lose out on Mr Right and you will be laying the foundations psychically for a successful relationship.

ASKING FOR A DATE

Now I know this probably sounds even more scary than introducing yourself. But you are an assertive woman, aren't you? And you don't want to let this guy slip through your fingertips, do you? Remember you are a powerful goddess, you are a confident woman and you like this man. He just feels right! So just casually ask him one of these questions:

'Would you like to go for a drink some time?'
'Have you got a pen so that I can give you my number?'
'Do you fancy going out for a coffee?'
'How can we make sure our paths cross again?'
'Fate has allowed me to meet you today, so how can we make sure we don't let her down by meeting again?'
'I sense we connect with each other on a spiritual level.

Would you like to go to an art gallery soon?'
'You have beautiful eyes. How can I make sure I can see them again?'
'I normally finish work around 6 p.m. Monday to Friday. Why don't we meet up one evening for a bite to eat?'

The list is endless and questions like these take the work out of thinking what to ask. Notice that they are also quite fun and not at all serious, which could put some guys off.

Getting Your Courage Up

If you are getting in a real flap about asking someone out, then nip to the loo or find a quiet space somewhere. Be positive and think about being bathed in white light, which will make you radiate positive energy.

Another great tip is to have a piece of quartz crystal in your bag or pocket, as this gives you strength and courage. You could charge it up before you go out. You do this by sitting alone holding the crystal. Imagine that it is filled with white light. Now it will be able to give you that extra bit of courage – very important when you are trying to set up a date.

———— * ————

Of course you might be in luck and he will ask you first. Unfortunately there is also the chance that he might turn you down. There could be many reasons for this, such as he already has a partner, he is gay, he is daft or he just doesn't fancy you (I know, how could he not, you're gorgeous).

This is not a problem, remember, it's a *challenge*. The challenge is to get it right next time. You will. Go home and sit at your love altar. Light your candles, burn your incense and ask that the slate be cleared for another attempt.

With all the wisdom you have gained, you should soon secure a date. By now you will have an idea of what you are looking for in a relationship and this date could be just the start. Now I want to look at what you should do on your first date. How will your newly awakened intuition and my fabulous rituals help you in the next phase of your love life?

Chapter 3
WHAT TO DO ON YOUR FIRST DATE

WITH ALL YOUR HARD WORK you should have a date now, right? The hard work isn't over, as we still have to secure a relationship out of this. What's the best way to go about making sure your first date goes so well that your guy is just dying to see you again?

The best night to start your relationship would be a Friday, as Venus, goddess of love, rules this day, so make sure you try to set up a date on a Friday. You must now prepare yourself so that you are ready to make the most of it.

PREPARATION

To begin with, just think about what you hope to get out of this first date. You want to make a good impression and for that eligible man to realise just how special you are. You want him to think about the possibilities of having you in his life. You also want to be able to listen to him and understand where he is coming from so that you can be sure you want him in your life.

You will need to be calm, though a first date is exciting and it is natural to be nervous. A very simple meditation will calm you down.

———————— * ————————

Meditation for Calm before a First Date

You will need:
* Lavender oil
* Patchouli oil

For this meditation, have some lavender and patchouli oil burning. I should get shares in lavender, the amount I use, and it is great for relaxation and soothing a troubled mind. Patchouli, on the other hand, is an aphrodisiac and helps you to feel warm waves of love. Together these will help to calm your mind and get your senses working.

In this meditation you want to be able to concentrate on two aspects of the date: *watching and listening*. Your eyes will be taking in so many signals about how the date is going and if you find the guy attractive, while your ears will be listening hard, as you don't want to miss a thing. We don't often think about it, but listening is an art form.

For this particular meditation you want to sit comfortably, either crossing your legs or kneeling. You should be on the floor, as this will ground you. Being grounded will also allow you to focus on your date and stop you from losing concentration or, even worse, interest.

So, sitting comfortably on the floor, close your eyes and breathe slowly. Allow your concentration to drift to your eyes and think about what a wonderful product of nature they are. What sort of things do you love to look at? For example, I love to see my children playing and laughing, so I would focus on that. What do you love to look at in particular with your wondrous eyes? Could it be a flower, perhaps an orchid of the most vivid pink? Think about what makes your eyes smile.

As you do this, also concentrate on your breathing. Listen to each breath as it comes in through your nose and out through your mouth and feel each breath as you draw it in and let it out.

Then turn your attention to your ears. What do you love to listen to? The sound of birds singing? In my case it is the great sound of my children laughing.

Now feel your body relax as you turn all your attention to your breathing, feeling your lungs fill with air and then expelling it slowly.

Do this for a few minutes then bring your senses back to the here and now. Feel happy in the knowledge that your senses are now tuned in to the wavelength of the coming date.

I would suggest doing this meditation before you start to get ready for the date. Being calm and aware will help you to make a success of the date.

GETTING READY

Of course you want the first date to go well. You want nature in all her glory to work with you and I have the perfect ritual to make this happen. My Scottish grannie told me about it before I went on my first date with my future husband. It is great fun and very effective. This ritual will help to tune you into the spiritual and natural world. It can't give any guarantees, but it will certainly help.

The first stage is to have a nice relaxing bath with oils such as ylang ylang and sandalwood. These will relax your body and mind. Also, wash your hair so that your whole body is cleansed. Doing this always helps a ritual to work better, as a build-up of dirt slows down the whole process. Cleansing the physical body also cleans the aura, which is the energy which surrounds our body, almost like an invisible bubble, and which is where we hold all our emotional baggage and worries. If the aura is clean then it is energised and ready to help us in our quest for love.

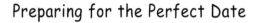

Preparing for the Perfect Date

You will need:
* 2 red candles
* 1 pink candle
* 3 silver-coloured candlesticks
* 2 rose quartz crystals
* Some dill

The red candles symbolise passion and the pink one pure romantic love. There are three candles as the number three in numerology signifies expansion and pushing things forward, so it is excellent for a first date. The rose quartz is the crystal of love and two of them represent two hearts coming together for the first time. Dill is a wonderful herb and I have loads of it in my herb garden. It is ruled by the planet Mercury and therefore in a ritual signifies a need for communication in all its forms. This will make him find you utterly irresistible.

Place the three candles on your altar and light them. Then put the two rose quartz crystals between them so that you have one red candle, then a rose quartz, then a pink candle and a rose quartz and finally the red candle.

Offer the dill up to the goddess of nature and ask her to help you on your date. You want it to be fun and to run smoothly. You also want to be calm and to stay in control.

Then, while thinking about how wonderful the date will be, say:

'*Goddess of nature, accept my gifts of crystals, dill and light. Make the date go great and keep love in sight.*'

This little ritual will set you up for the date and help you feel confident.

———*———

PRESENTATION

How you present yourself on your date is very important. You want to make a good impression, so that your man realises just why he is on a date with you. So you need to think about what to wear, how to ensure you are well groomed, what your voice sounds like and how you should act on the date itself. Think of yourself as a package which has to be attractive. Don't go out looking like a dog's dinner – take some time over getting your appearance right. On my first date with Ronald I wore a black suit and a jade green top. These colours signified expanding my horizons, which was certainly the message I wanted to convey.

WHAT TO WEAR?

Once you have this decision out of the way you will feel much more relaxed about the whole date. My rule of thumb is that you should dress in a way which will make you feel relaxed. By that I mean don't wear something which will leave you feeling self-conscious and distract you from the job in hand. You don't want to wear a skirt so short that you spend all night stretching it over your knees.

Make sure that what you decide to wear flatters you. If you have great legs, then show them off. If you have a great bust, then wear a top which accentuates your figure.

From a psychic point of view, you should be able to sense what will be appropriate for the date. Just tap into your psychic ability as we did earlier (*see pages 51–54*). Let your intuition guide you and you will choose the perfect first date outfit. Another asset is a good friend who gives you honest advice on what suits you.

What Colours to Wear on Your Date

I set great store by colour. My life has always been filled with colour and if you saw my mum then you would know where it came from. She wears dazzling colours and on a dull day she can light up the darkest room. Colour makes me smile when I am feeling low and calms me down when I feel nervous. And on a first date the importance of colour cannot be underestimated. It sends out so many signals that it is essential to get it right.

On a psychic level, colour also plays an important part in helping you tune into your Higher Self. This is because each colour has an individual energy vibration. Each of these vibrations affects the chakras, the energy centres in the body. The energies of violet, blue or turquoise help to tune in your psychic awareness.

Colour has the amazing ability to alter mood, which is perfect for your date. Bright colours such as purple and turquoise cheer us up. Drab colours such as grey or khaki can make us uninspired and slow physically. For your date the following six colours are the best to wear, as they can bring an extra bit of psychic help to the proceedings. You only have to wear a splash of the colour for it to work:

Blue This is the colour of healing. It calms the mind and is best used on a date where your nerves may get the better of you. It is also helpful if you are carrying around a lot of emotional baggage. On a date it will help keep the hurt of past relationships at bay. As already mentioned, it encourages communication, which will also be useful on your date.

Green This, as I have said before, is the colour I wore on my first date with my husband. Green is the colour of nature and it gives a feeling of connection with the natural world. It is also symbolic of trees and life itself, so reveals that in your relationship you are looking for abundance. The connecting with nature also helps you to keep your feet on the ground during the date.

Orange This colour is great for lifting the spirits and will affect both the person wearing it and those around them. It is a healing colour that brings warmth just like a ray of sunshine. If you have any aches or pains, orange's warm healing energy will help to relieve them.

Pink All shades of pink bring about a feeling of warmth and safety. It is a secure colour which allows love to grow. It also reflects romance in its most pure form. If it is romance you are looking for, then wear pink on the date.

Red This colour is a stimulant to us. Physically, it quickens our heartbeat and has the effect of increasing adrenaline around the body. It therefore excites us psychologically and is seen to encourage passion. It is linked to the element fire. You don't have to dress from head to toe in it, but a little splash on a scarf or even a top would be enough to signal passion.

White This colour shows that as a person you have nothing to hide. You are an open book and what you see is what you get. As the colour of purity it also reveals that you are a person of high morals, so there will be no hanky panky on the first date!

What colour are you going to choose? Use your intuition to pick one. Also, go for a colour that suits you and that you feel comfortable with. If you are a redhead and you feel pink is the colour for you but that it would clash with your locks, just put a pink hanky in your pocket. It will work just as well.

On my first date, as I mentioned, I wore black with green. Black is a good colour to wear as it sets off the other colours and helps to absorb their energy.

To make it easier for you to decide on a colour, I would suggest doing the following exercise.

---- * ----

Choosing a Colour

You will need:
* Felt tip pens
* White pen
* White paper
* Black paper
* Pair of scissors

With the scissors cut the white paper into five squares. On each square choose a colour and write the word in the colour, for example write 'red' in red. Do this for the colours given on pages 99–100. For white, use the white pen on the black paper.

Then fold the squares up and place them in front of you on a table. Close your eyes and ask to be guided which colour to pick.

Then slowly pass your left hand, which is your intuitive one, over the pieces of paper. Friends and family who have done this have felt a tingle or just knew that a particular paper was the one to choose.

Choose your paper, then open your eyes and see which one it is.

This is great fun to do and I am sure you will be happy with the result.

———————*———————

HOW WELL GROOMED ARE YOU?

When I think of the word 'groomed' I can't help thinking of a dog. But I am here to make sure that you are the belle of the ball, or the date, so take grooming seriously. It simply means getting yourself neat and tidy – and that includes your clothes, hair, nails and even your shoes. The whole package is really important.

Moving from head to toe, before the date make sure that you are happy with the way your hair looks. If you aren't, then book an appointment with the hairdresser and go for either a restyle or a touch up. If your hair looks good, it will help you feel good on the date.

Your nails are also important as our hands say a lot about us. In spite of this they are often overlooked. When I first met Ronald I had nails so long that I could hardly pull up zips or undo buttons. In fact on our first date I could hardly lift the first drink he bought me as the glass kept sliding out of my hands. To avoid this sort of thing, treat yourself to a manicure before the date. Again, it will help you to relax and raise your confidence levels.

Your feet are another area many of us don't think about. The shoes you wear on the date are important as they reflect your personality. Safe flat pumps or sexy high heels, the choice is yours. Just be sure you are giving the message you want to.

Another important aspect of your shoes is whether you can actually walk in them. A very good friend of mine once went on a date in brand new £450 Jimmy Choo designer sandals. They were so high she could hardly walk in them. Her date was in a very posh restaurant in Chelsea and it went pearshaped when she got up to go to the little girl's room. Her heels got caught on the wrought iron stairs down to the toilet and she fell over and broke her ankle and the heels of her shoes and, worst of all, flashed her bright red thong to the whole restaurant. Her romance is still on, but it might not have been after such a shaky start.

YOUR VOICE

Your voice is the blueprint of who you are. It is what distinguishes you at a distance or allows you to be heard close up in a crowd. Make sure that on your date your voice is clear so that you can get your message across.

Another pearl of wisdom my grandmother told me was to think just before I spoke. This is important when on a date as you will be nervous and you don't want to say something you might later regret. Also be yourself and don't put on an accent. You will only be found out in the end and imagine the embarrassment.

If you are a bit on the shy side or you just want to make sure that your voice is strong and clear on the date then I have a great trick you can use.

————*————

Strengthening Your Voice

Stand in front of a mirror which is big enough to give you a full view of your head and shoulders.

Take a yellow scarf or piece of material and wrap it around your neck.

Then say: 'Oh lami, oh lama.'

Say this three times and sense the vibrations in your throat.

This is a traditional Turkish way to make the voice strong and the holy men who call the faithful to prayers may well use it. The colour yellow is significant as it is related to Mercury, the planet of communication.

————*————

YOUR PERFUME

How you smell is another important way for your date to size you up. Naturally you want to create a good impression. Go for a perfume with jasmine, ylang ylang, rose, patchouli and/or geranium in it. These are all linked to the senses and to vibrations of romance, so are important in a successful date. They also mimic female sex hormones, which should help him feel passionate.

Bear in mind, however, that it's not good to wear anything overpowering which might make your date sneeze or feel queasy. A work colleague of mine once went out on a date with a guy who was a real drip in the real sense of the word. She wore a lovely Estée Lauder perfume which made his nose stream all night long. The relationship didn't get over the first hurdle.

HOW TO KEEP CALM

I can assure you that your first date will be nerve-racking. What I can do is show you simple methods and a ritual to help you keep your boots extra chilled.

RELAX

Hopefully you will have had a couple of good nights' sleep before the date. To make extra sure you do, have lavender baths and put lavender oil on your pillow so that you sleep like a baby. Beauty sleep is just so important.

Just before the date itself you should have a nice relaxing bath. Adding lavender oil to the bath and having some lavender candles, soft music and a glass of wine will all help you chill. Make sure you stay in the bath and switch yourself off from the outside world so you get the benefit of the oil and ambience. Once you have had your bath you could rub lavender body lotion onto your skin so that the benefits of this relaxing herb stay with you during the date.

THINK POSITIVELY

To keep your mind focused and calm, remember to breathe slowly. Listen to your breath. As you do you will feel peace flowing over you. Meditating before you get dressed will also relax you. Try the following.

———————*———————

Relaxing Meditation

Sitting on the floor, think about the colour purple. Close your eyes and imagine that you are covered in a purple velvet cloak. This will give you a feeling of calm and positive vibes about the date.

Then open your eyes, get up from the floor and get ready for the date. You will enjoy it, just keep telling yourself you will!

———————*———————

LAUGH

Laughter will help you to release the tension that you will be feeling. So, to stop nerves getting the better of you, take some time to watch a comedy before going out or phone a friend who makes you laugh.

CARRY A 'DATE BAG'

The 'date bag' is my version of a lucky charm bag my old Turkish grannie passed on to me. I used it on my very first date with Ronald and I am sure it helped things run smoothly.

The bag can be any style or colour. What should you carry in it? First, place a rose quartz crystal inside. This will help to raise the psychic flow of love between the two of you. Then put in a small piece of pink paper or card with the word 'Venus' written on it in red pen to evoke the love goddess and enhance your love.

———

Also, don't forget breath freshener and your perfume. These will keep your breath and body smelling sweet. Your emergency make-up pack of lipstick, concealer, powder and eye shadow should mean that your face doesn't let you down no matter how sticky or sweaty things get. Notepaper is another good idea, as is a pen so that you can jot down any important details like your mobile phone number.

How to Handle the Date

When the date is about to start you are bound to feel nervous – that is perfectly normal. You may even feel sick. But you've done your rituals and you are all ready. You even have the goddess of love on your side and the most powerful forces of nature working on your behalf. So don't worry. Just remember the five golden rules to a successful first date:

1. Positive initial contact.

2. Chilling out.

3. Keeping up the flow of information.

4. Catching and keeping your date's attention.

5. Feasting on the rewards!

POSITIVE INITIAL CONTACT

Be on time for your date as this is always a good omen for the future happiness of the relationship. Present yourself well – stand up straight, shoulders back, not slouching. If his first sight of you is as an upright, strong and confident woman, that's a good start.

With any luck you will meet your date as planned. You can either greet him with a friendly kiss on both cheeks as the Europeans do or, if you don't feel comfortable with that, you can just shake hands. Touch is so important at this point as it allows you to connect with your new date on a more spiritual and personal level. Your greeting should be the start of a great time together, no matter how long that may be. So smile and make sure that you are making good eye contact. This positive body language will let him know that you are pleased to see him.

At first you will be adjusting to one another, so don't start any heavy topics of conversation. Just engage in idle chatter about things such as your journey to the date or that old chestnut, the weather. Just get to know how it feels to be in his presence at this stage. It should feel non-threatening and comfortable.

CHILLING OUT

This normally happens when you have both arrived at the destination of the date, perhaps a restaurant, cinema or bar. You should now start to relax and enjoy the date. Your conversation should still be non-threatening, but now aim to find out more about your date, for example what his holiday plans are or where he lives and whether he likes it. Keep it light – you can ask more detailed questions later on. Make him feel that you already have a good idea who he is and what he's all about. He will probably ask you questions, too, hopefully in a relaxed manner.

If you really fancy your date, you may want to play with your hair, even tousling it and touching your neck. In body language terms this means that you are a sexual being and you want another person to respond to you. If you really want to get this across, keep saying in your head, 'I am sexy, I am sexy!'

A little booze will help you relax, but just make sure you don't get too drunk. I knew a girl who took chilling out on a date to a whole new level. She got so drunk within the first half hour of the date that by the time they moved on to a restaurant she puked up her starter all over the table. Not glamorous or clever! So don't go mad, just stay cool and enjoy the company.

KEEPING UP THE FLOW OF INFORMATION

By this point your main objective is to discover as much viable information about your date as possible. This is essential if you want to seriously consider him as a future partner. You also want to suss out whether or not you are compatible.

Here are some stock questions to ask. You may have asked some of them already – they can come up at any point in the date – and you may know some of the answers already. But these five questions should give you a rough idea about the person sitting in front of you:

'What kind of work is it you do?'
'How do you spend your leisure time?'

'Are you from a big or small family?'
'Where is your favourite destination for a holiday?'
'Where are you living at the moment?'

Obviously your date will want to know lots about you as well. Answer as honestly as you can. The flow of information will give you both a chance to think about how compatible you are.

———————— * ————————

Checking Honesty

To make sure that your date is being honest, a very easy tip is to visualise a set of scales as you ask your questions and answer his. The scales represent the sign of Libra, which brings about equality and truthfulness. They may tip one way or the other. Then, when your date is over or you feel content that the truth is being told, you can stop the image in your head. Very simple, but another great tip from Ruth the Truth!

———————— * ————————

CATCHING AND KEEPING YOUR DATE'S ATTENTION

By this stage either the date will be going really well and you will want to capture his heart or you will have realised that he is not going to be the one for you. For now we will assume that all is going well. Later we will deal with the 'date from hell'. But now let's say that by this point you are really very interested in a full relationship with this man.

Your date bag is working, communication is flowing and psychically your instincts are telling you that he could be part of your life.

To catch your fish, do the following:

1. Be natural.

2. Make sure you let him know that you are interested. Look attentive and enthusiastic.

3. Laugh, even if he is telling silly or rotten jokes.

4. Make him feel desirable by using your body language wisely – for example, touch his arm, tousle your hair, smile at him and give lots of eye contact.

5. Be chilled.

6. Make sure you are showing a little bit of cleavage and just a little bit of leg. Leave him gagging for more.

All of these will make him want you. You just have to be honest and open. No pretences. Just be upfront and proud of it.

FEASTING ON THE REWARDS!

As the date comes to an end you should both be left wanting more. Take things slowly, as a new relationship will thrive on the mantra 'Love slow, live long'. I suggest that if the vibes feel right then a good old snog never goes amiss. But should you go any further? Remember you want him to respect you, not think you are some raving hussy.

Do, however, make sure you organise another date before you part company. Then say your goodbyes. Hopefully you will have a gooey warm feeling in your stomach.

When you get back home, go to your love altar, light a red candle and just give thanks for this special person entering your life.

WHAT IF THE DATE GOES PEARSHAPED!

So, OK, you meet him and find he is just not what you expected. Or he's downright rude. Or you get a case of projectile vomiting. A very close family member of mine found she was out with a Jekyll and Hyde character who had a habit of shouting midway through sentences. That was bad enough, but she then ordered a soup which was billed as vegetarian and wasn't. She was so dismayed to discover she had eaten a large bit of ham that she promptly had a case of projectile vomiting. As you can imagine, the date ended quickly and at 10.30 p.m. that night she was calling me for advice.

I told this person to do the following ritual and it is a wee cracker. It helped her and it can help you too. If you have had a bad date, then do it. It will clear the way for a new love interest to come into your life. Remember, a bad date is not the end of the world and there are plenty more fish in the sea.

---- ✳ ----

Recovery from a Pearshaped Date

You will need:
* White candle
* Silver-coloured candlestick
* Happy photo of yourself
* Pear that's ready to eat
* Piece of white paper and a black pen
* Pyrex dish

For this I want you to sit down and think about the date. I know that this might be difficult, especially if it was traumatic, but just write down the main things which went wrong.

Now light the candle and use it to burn the paper safely in a Pyrex dish or the sink, where it can be safely extinguished. As you do this, think about the fact that you are banishing all the negativity you have experienced.

Focus on your photo and think about how happy you will feel when you eventually meet the man of your dreams.

Then, as a symbol of your triumph over adversity, take the pear and eat it. Yes, you know the date went wrong, but you are not going to dwell on it. You have overcome another obstacle in your life.

After all of this, stand up and dust yourself down. Start by brushing your head and arms with your hands, then your torso, legs and finally your feet. Dust the negative vibes away. You will live to see another day.

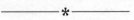

So you have survived that bumpy and fraught ride of a first date. If it didn't work out, never mind, try and try again until you do meet Mr Right. If it did go well, then read on. The next chapter will show you how to move on to develop a wonderful relationship. There's so much to look forward to!

Chapter 4
MOVING ON FROM THE FIRST DATE

WITH THE FIRST DATE OVER and the second a possibility, it is now time to turn our attention to communication. So many people write to my columns every week with their relationships facing crisis. Normally the problem is the 'C' word, as I call it – communication. If you don't communicate with your lover, then how is he supposed to know what you want out of the relationship?

Communication has moved on since I was dating Ronald in the 1980s. We now have a whole range of options, including mobile phones, pagers and computers. Of course the ordinary landline phone is still in use, but there is so much choice now as to how we get in touch. In this book I have endeavoured to highlight traditional methods of bringing love into your life. But we must also make provision for new technology. If you were to send your lover a letter through the post you would hope to get your point across. I believe that this same point could be made just as easily using a text message from a mobile phone. There is still a flow of energy there. This chapter will allow you to discover the magic which can be found in both traditional and modern ways of communication.

First I want you to try a lovely ritual my Scottish gran taught me in the early stages of my relationship with Ronald. It is to help with those early days. I know it works, as it did for me.

————— * —————

Looking Forward

You will need:
* 1 magnet or lodestone
* 1 red pouch or purse
* 1 needle
* Dark red thread

Carry this out on a New Moon, as this will be good energy for the growth of your new relationship. The time you should perform it should be a multiple of six, the number associated with love magic, so 6 p.m., 12 p.m. and so on. In numerology six is the number which governs relationships, so it is more than apt here.

Take the red pouch and put the lodestone or magnet in it. Then use the needle and thread to sew up the opening to seal the crystal magnet inside.

Sit quietly and think about your boyfriend. Imagine that he is in love with you and that you both agree that this is a good and positive thing. Close your eyes, hold the pouch and say, 'Lover, stay with me so that we can grow.'

The best thing to do is to keep the pouch with you at all times, especially when you are together. The magnet signifies his attraction for you and is symbolic of the beginning of the relationship.

———————*———————

This ritual works really slowly, so it is perfect for the early period of a relationship. It also, as I certainly discovered, helps the path of true love to run smoothly.

BEING HONEST

Being yourself is of prime importance and it really determines the type of soul mate you will attract. From the first date you need to have a policy of honesty and openness. This doesn't mean that during your first couple of meetings you should spill your guts and tell him everything that has happened in your life, especially not the heavy stuff. A time will come when this is appropriate, but at the beginning it should be kept light.

BEING HONEST WITH YOURSELF

You also need to be really honest with yourself. Is this person really who you are looking for? Tune into your Higher Self for guidance and listen to your inner voice. What is it telling you? Is it positive? Does it feel right? The following meditation will help you with this.

————*————

Consulting Your Higher Self

You will need:
* Pink tourmaline
* Clear quartz

Sit in a peaceful setting and take the pink tourmaline in your left hand and the clear quartz in your right hand. Pink tourmaline helps in tuning in to the vibrations associated with love and therefore how you feel. The clear quartz helps to focus your mind and ground you.

Close your eyes and ask your Higher Self to guide you in the relationship you have just embarked on. You may hear your inner voice speaking to you or see images. Take note of all the information you receive, as it will be relevant to your present situation.

Once you have finished, open your eyes and thank your Higher Self for its assistance.

————*————

ARE YOU HEADING IN THE RIGHT DIRECTION?

So, it is still early days in your relationship but you want to know if you are heading in the right direction. The dates you have been on are good. You have common interests. You probably both reckon that you are compatible, but how certain can you be?

I once met a very old, very psychic lady on a television programme on which I was a guest. All her life she had carried out readings using nothing more than a basic pack of playing cards, and she showed me how. The following is my interpretation of her oracle. It is great to use just to see if you are in the right ballpark in your relationship. I have an in-depth love oracle in Chapter 7, but this is just a simple one which has given good advice to my friends and family. It is another way of seeing if you are going in the correct direction.

'Is He Right for Me?' Oracle

You will need:
* New pack of playing cards
* Red pouch or scarf
* Rose quartz
* Clear quartz

You can do this on your own or in the company of friends. If you do it with a glass of wine, some nibbles and on a Friday night, even better.

Sit quietly and ask to be given a sign that your new man is worth the effort.

Take the new pack of playing cards and remove the suit of hearts. Place this suit in the red pouch or scarf with a rose quartz for love and clear quartz for clarity and leave it for an hour to be charged up with positive colour and crystal energy. During this time enjoy being with friends or, if you are on your own, keep yourself busy. Just don't dwell on the cards; chill out as best you can. Also, remember not to take this too seriously – it should be used as just a gentle guide.

When the hour is up, remove the cards from the red covering. As you do this, close your eyes and imagine that you are covered in a brilliant white light. This will protect you from any harmful energies.

Then shuffle the cards, making sure you put your imprint on them. If you have friends with you they can do this as well.

Next imagine that your third eye, which is in the middle of your forehead, is opening up and that psychic energy is moving between it and the cards.

Now open your eyes. You are charged with psychic energy.

Take the cards in your hands and feel them. Then start to shuffle them. Ask: 'Is this man worth the effort?' Choose one card with your right hand for your answer.

The following is what each card means.

Ace of Hearts Great aspects – go for it!

Two of Hearts Work on your communication and things will improve.

Three of Hearts He may need more work than you expect.

Four of Hearts Honesty will be important for it to work.

Five of Hearts This will have difficulty working as a personality clash is possible.

Six of Hearts Is this lust or love? Think about it.

Seven of Hearts The relationship needs work on a basic level, starting with communication.

Eight of Hearts You are well matched, even spiritually.

Nine of Hearts Distance may eventually cause problems.

Ten of Hearts Happy times are ahead.

Page of Hearts An obstacle is just ahead. Work on it and things will be fine.

Queen of Hearts You've met your soul mate.

King of Hearts Don't let money or power come between you.

Once you have your answer, accept that it is for guidance only. After all, you are your own person, aren't you?

———— * ————

When I was first married I had my friends and sisters over to the house for a wine and nibbles night. We all did the oracle, taking turns. As each of us took our messages from the cards one of my sisters chose the Page of Hearts, 'An obstacle is just ahead. Work on it and things will be fine.' Two weeks later her boyfriend got a job a long way away. They worked at it and are happily married today.

METHODS OF COMMUNICATION

I am going to concentrate here on modern ways of communication such as sending e-mails and text messages.

Traditional ways such as phone calls and letters will be dealt with to a lesser degree. We will look at these first, though, as for many of us they are still the main ways of communicating with our loved ones.

LETTER WRITING

Now I know that you are sitting there saying, 'Letter writing? Who, me?!' Well, not everyone has access to a computer and writing is the perfect opportunity to get feelings down on paper. You could even be a CCS – compulsive card sender. They do live in our midst. I have friends who send cards at the drop of a hat and it is great as a mark of friendship.

When trying to build on a romance letters and cards need to be written with great thought and skill. There may be things you want to say that you just can't bring yourself to say in person. Letter writing is a beautiful way to communicate.

The following is a very simple ritual that you can do when you write letters to someone very special in your life. An old aunt of mine told me about it when I was courting and when I did it I found my letters took on a life of their own. Also, Ronald seemed to know exactly what I was talking about. Two days after he had received my first letter, a large bunch of roses was sent to my home. Ronald had written the most romantic poem on the card. If this can work for me, just imagine what it could do for you.

———————*———————

Writing a Love Letter

You will need:
* Really good-quality pink paper
* Blue pen
* Red ribbon
* His favourite perfume

For this you want to use the best paper money can buy. The colour pink is important as it signifies love and happiness, which of course is your ultimate goal. A blue pen is also important here as blue relates to all types of communication, especially the written word.

Sit down quietly and think about what you want to write. What do you want the tone of your letter to be? Let your mind, spirit and emotions bring you to the place you want to be heard from. Then let your psychic flow direct you to write your letter of love and understanding.

Once you have finished, take his favourite perfume, one that he loves to smell on you, and spray it onto the letter so that when he opens the envelope his first thought is of you and how wonderful you are.

Once you have done that, fold the letter over and tie the red ribbon around it in a lovely bow. The red ribbon will seal the spirit of the letter and all it communicates so that it doesn't get diluted in the post, so to speak. Then put the letter in the envelope and get it ready to post.

As you post it, say, 'Letter filled with words of love, make my sweetheart understand my heart.'

This is a lovely ritual and I am so glad that my old aunt passed on her wisdom to me.

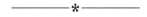

Letters are a wonderful non-threatening way to communicate with your loved one. Next I want to look at how we can make the ordinary phone an instrument of romantic communication.

THE PHONE

I know that you will be thinking that I have really lost the plot now, devoting time and energy to the simple phone. But think about it. How long do you spend talking to your boyfriend on the phone? Ages, I bet, and here is a record for you to ponder. When I was first going out with Ronald we were once on the phone from 7 p.m. to 3 a.m. My mum's phone bill can vouch for this.

Every time you phone someone or they phone you, you are giving out energy. Mostly this will be positive, but on the odd occasion it will be negative. This could be because you are not happy with how the conversation is going or it could be that you feel frustrated, as you can't get your point across. How do you make sure that the other person is getting the message? For a start you can think about what you want to talk about before you even pick up the phone.

Preparing to Phone

Take a few breaths just to relax and close your eyes, imagining your communication as a river. Imagine it starting as a spring in beautiful heather-laden hills and getting stronger and stronger until it becomes a river. Think about the words that you want to communicate and your psychic flow will connect with you like a river and allow the communication to progress.

On a practical level, make sure that you are sitting comfortably during your call and that you have a hand free to hold a citrine quartz crystal. If you don't have a hand free, then put the citrine quartz beside you. It will help to stimulate your mind and keep you alert during your conversation. It will also assist memory recall so that there is no chance that you will forget all the things you want to talk about.

From this moment on all phone calls will have a new meaning for you.

NEW METHODS OF COMMUNICATION

Everywhere you go nowadays you will see people talking on their mobile phones. Not only talking, but texting too. Computers are another new way of communicating with our friends, family and loved ones. I get around 70–80 e-mails a day that need a response. So when you are starting out on your relationship, you must consider these modern methods of communication. But how can you get spiritual and connected using a mobile phone or a computer? Is there any technological magic we can use to help us in our search for love?

Mobile Phones and Texting

The same rules apply to the mobile phone as to the normal landline phone. If you keep your citrine quartz crystal in your pocket it will help the flow of communication as you walk about talking on your mobile phone.

Texting is a whole different ball game. It is quick and is ideal for getting your point across in a plain and simple way. Where magic is concerned it is great too, as the spells are fast and down to earth.

Why not try the following text ritual? It is perfect for just after your first date, especially when you know that something special is happening between you. Its main focus is to allow the text message to get to the recipient with a big splurge of positive energy. It also helps you to get what you are saying across. You want him to get the message, right?

I have a confession to make. I have done this one without Ronald knowing about it and each time he has told me how great he feels when he receives the message. He said it is 'like getting a tingly feeling through the phone'. A very good friend of mine who had been looking for love for some time tried it out too and is now engaged to the guy. So if you want to jazz up your relationship, why not try it? Oh and it is great fun too!

------------*------------

Sending Loving Vibes via a Text Message

You will need:
* Mobile phone
* Citrine quartz
* Yellow ribbon
* Yellow candle

What I want you to do is to take your mobile phone and place it on your love altar. Put the yellow candle in the middle of your altar, then light it. As you do, imagine warming rays of the Sun coming down and saturating the mobile phone with its yellow light.

Hold the citrine quartz in your right hand and feel its positive vibes. Then pick up your mobile phone with your left hand. This will charge the phone up with your psychic vibes so that when you next text it will be a really positive experience.

The ribbon should be tied around the phone safely to keep the energy flow going after you finish the ritual. The knot you make in the ribbon will also seal the ritual and keep it working.

Yellow is the colour we are focusing on here, as it is the colour of positive energy, which is what we are trying to send in our text message. It is the colour of the Sun's rays, which always bring happiness. In colour therapy yellow also has a high vibrational value, so it lifts the spirits. Try this ritual and check out the amazing response.

It is also important to look after your mobile phone and keep it clean and well cared for, especially when you are carrying it around with you. Treat it with respect, as it is an instrument of love communication.

E-mail

E-mail seems to be the fastest growing method of communication for many people on the planet right now, whether it's business or personal interaction. E-mailing is simple, quick and in no time at all you can get a reply. You can bet that if you and your new love interest both have access to a computer soon after your first date you will be sending e-mails to each other. In no time at all your little black book will have his home number, mobile number and e-mail address.

How can we make such a technical approach to communication more spiritual and psychic? Well, that is where I come into the equation. Just take my tried and tested advice and I am convinced you will see results.

To start with we need to concentrate on your computer area. It needs to become a sacred shrine where peace and harmony reign. Computers, like most forms of electrical equipment, have a very strong electromagnetic field. These negative energies build up and can lead to headaches, tension, irritability and a host of other problems. Before you send e-mails, especially any relating to your new and hopefully thriving relationship, you need to neutralise the negative effects of the computer.

I suggest you have a nice piece of amethyst crystal and a piece of clear quartz next to your computer. The amethyst has the ability to take away the heavy charged atmosphere caused by computers and leave you with a better quality of air. Amethyst is also a healing crystal for the mind and it will calm you when you are not feeling your best. The clear quartz gives you clarity of vision and thought. I can promise that if you have these nearby you will notice the energy field around the computer lightening up.

You could also put a purple cloth near to where you use your computer. Purple is a healing colour and it will strengthen the positive vibes around you. I did all this when I first started working from home and it was actually my husband who commented on how the room felt much less charged.

Before sending e-mails to your loved one, think about what you are going to say. Then take a blue candle and light it near to you but away from where it could cause damage to the computer. This will ease the flow of communication as you think, type and send the e-mail.

If your first date was great, send an e-mail saying so. Even add that you can't wait until you have the chance to do the same again. As you send it, imagine it is travelling through cyberspace with a white guiding light taking it to your special person's heart.

I developed a ritual for a friend of mine who had difficulty putting her point across to her new boyfriend via e-mail. Afterwards she found that the love energy improved and he realised what she was really trying to say.

———— * ————

E-mail Ritual for Clarifying Your Thoughts

If you think about it, using a computer is just using a lot of symbols that someone can understand. Throughout history symbolism has brought us in tune with our Higher Spiritual Self. A computer can also be thought of in this way.

Go into your computer so that you can save the document you are about to type. Save it as 6LOVE.

In the new document I want you to type in six rows of the number six. Then type in six rows of the capital letter O. Finally type in three wise owls ^oo^ just like this.   v

Your finished document should look something like this:

666666666666666666666666666666666666666666666666
666666666666666666666666666666666666666666666666
666666666666666666666666666666666666666666666666
666666666666666666666666666666666666666666666666
666666666666666666666666666666666666666666666666
666666666666666666666666666666666666666666666666
OOOOOOOOOOOOOOOOOOOOOOOOOOOOOOOOOOOOOOOOOO
OOOOOOOOOOOOOOOOOOOOOOOOOOOOOOOOOOOOOOOOOO
OOOOOOOOOOOOOOOOOOOOOOOOOOOOOOOOOOOOOOOOOO
OOOOOOOOOOOOOOOOOOOOOOOOOOOOOOOOOOOOOOOOOO
OOOOOOOOOOOOOOOOOOOOOOOOOOOOOOOOOOOOOOOOOO
OOOOOOOOOOOOOOOOOOOOOOOOOOOOOOOOOOOOOOOOOO

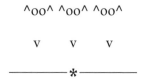

^oo^ ^oo^ ^oo^

v   v   v

———————*———————

I know it looks crazy, but just stick with me on this one. The symbolism in this document is powerful and it activates your computer to be used as a communication tool for love and understanding.

The number six signifies love in numerology and the six rows serve to make the love between you and your loved one stronger. The capital O relates to the Full Moon, which gives us complete emotional stability. It also allows us to understand the issues involved in a love affair. The wise owl, which is my favourite bit in all of this, gives you wisdom and knowledge in your relationship. In animal symbolism the owl has always represented wisdom. There are three owls here as three represents life itself, as in a mother, father and child, so this gives inner wisdom for the lifetime of the relationship.

Once you have finished the document in all its glory, save it and send it to your loved one. You only need to do it this once as the psychic energy is now within the workings of your computer. This will allow the computer to be used as a tool of communication in love.

The friend I developed this for thought I was mad suggesting it, but as I had been right about most things in the past, she did it. Two days later I got an e-mail from her praising my ingenious idea, as the e-mails she was sending and receiving just seemed to say much more. She wrote: 'It is as if I now know what he is trying to tell me and I can express myself much more clearly.' So keep saying to yourself, 'My computer is a tool of love, my computer is a tool of love . . .'

A final word of advice about e-mails: when you have quarrels, as we always do in relationships, don't send an e-mail. If you are anything like me, you will write things you don't mean and then once you have sent the e-mail you will feel bad. My advice is to go away, have a coffee and calm down, then go back to the computer.

ASKING FOR HELP
IN COMMUNICATION

There will be times, especially at the beginning of a relationship, when you can't express your feelings easily. This may be because you don't know the person well enough or aren't sure of his values. It can be a difficult and awkward time and things can go wrong. This needn't be the case, though. Why not ask for help from your spiritual guides? On the long and rocky road to love I believe you need all the help that you can get.

An example I can give of help from the spirit world is last year when my dear friend Anna passed away with breast cancer. I tried to contact her just to check that she was OK in the other realm. Anna came through quite flustered and she told me she was really busy looking after a baby's well-being on the Earth plane. She was polite, as always, but said the baby was a member of the family and asked me to leave her alone until her important work was finished. I must admit I was confused, as to the best of my knowledge there were no babies in her family. I relayed the message to Anna's sister, who didn't understand it either. The next day, though, she discovered that a niece was pregnant but that there were concerns over the baby. She phoned me up immediately and I was glad I had finally got to the heart of the mystery. I am also glad to report that the baby was born safe and well; due, I have no doubt, to Anna's support.

To connect with your spirit guides, you can use the exercises given in the first chapter (*see pages 44–66*) or you might like to try my five-point plan. This always works for me and I have taught it to many people who are not necessarily as psychic as I am. The steps are clear and simple.

———— * ————

How to Connect with Your Spirit Guides

1. Begin by psychically protecting yourself. Sit quietly, making sure you are comfortable, and close your eyes. Imagine that you are immersed in golden light. This will protect you, ensuring only positive energy can enter your aura.

2. Relax your body and your mind will follow. As you close your eyes, tense your head and shoulders, hold for a count of five and then relax. Feel these parts of your body becoming heavier and more relaxed. Then take your thoughts to your arms and stomach. Tense these parts, hold for a count of five, then relax. Feel the heaviness and let all the stress just float away. Finally tense your legs and feet then relax them. You will find that your body feels more at peace after this.

3. Now concentrate on your breathing. This will quieten your mind and get rid of all the day's business which is swirling around your head. Breathe in for a count of four, then out for four. Listen to each breath going in then out.

Focus on this and only this. Do this for at least five minutes. You will find your mind relaxing and slowing down.

4. You now need to raise your energy vibrations so that you can make contact with your spirit guides. To do this you must use creative visualisation. As you sit comfortably with your eyes closed I want you to imagine that you are in a bubble of white light. The light can become brighter or dimmer at the push of a button and as it gets brighter the vibrations around you will increase. Now I know this is a strange concept, but just trust me, it works. As the light gets brighter and your energy vibrations increase, you will be able to sense your spirit guides. It will take time and practice, so be patient, but you can do it. You may see them or hear what they have to say or sense them in some other way.

5. Once you have made your connection, your spirit guides will help you, so it is good to have questions at the ready. For example, ask how you can best communicate with your lover or whether their values are the same as yours. You will sense the answers in some way. You may hear a voice speaking in your mind, either a familiar one or one you don't know. You may see colours, visions or images. Your emotions may also be an indication of your communication with your guides. Take note of these. Everything you experience during this time will build a picture of your contact with your guides.

Once you have finished, thank your guides for the connection and ask them to help you again at a later date. Then press your imaginary button and dim the lights. Open your eyes and feel grateful for all the help you have been offered.

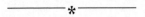

I taught this five-point plan to a lady who had came to me asking how she could learn to communicate better in her new relationship. Her marriage had ended in divorce and all because she just couldn't express her feelings. I was amazed three weeks later when she called to say that she had made contact with her spirit guide, who was a Native American called Strong Red River, and he gave her wisdom which answered her questions. She just couldn't believe it when she visualised this large Native American, but he helped her make a real go of her new relationship. She felt that she was being cared for not just on this Earth but also on the spiritual plane and that made her feel good.

This can work for you too, so try it and see who is guiding you. In time you will learn to connect with your spirit guides just by closing your eyes and they will give you answers to your questions.

Communication in all its forms should definitely be easier now, even on your computer! Technology can become a part of any ritual and I have proved it.

By now you will have realised that you have found someone very special, someone you can relate to and whose company you really enjoy. So how you can move from the puppy dog love to a deeper, more spiritual love?

Chapter 5
BUILDING YOUR RELATIONSHIP

LOVE IS A BEAUTIFUL THING and when you are in the throes of it life can feel absolutely brilliant. When I first went out with Ronald I could hardly sleep for weeks with the excitement of it all. Above all, I want you to enjoy this time. You have worked hard and deserve it. I know that the journey has not been an easy one. The path to true love never is, I suppose, unless you are very lucky.

Finding someone special is cause for great celebration and I have a ritual to show the powers that be how thankful we are. I perform it once a month to thank my lucky stars that I met Ronald, the true love of my life. It was an old ritual which was passed down from my Turkish family and it has worked for us for many centuries. It comes from the mountains of southern Turkey, where rituals and magic are often part of people's everyday lives. It is excellent for giving thanks and is therefore great for thanking the universe for your special love.

---*---

To Celebrate Your Love

You will need:
* Fresh pink and red rose petals (not dried)
* Glass bowl full of water
* 2 white candles
* 2 silver-coloured candlesticks
* Jasmine essential oil
* Rose quartz crystal

This ritual should be performed on the night of the Full Moon. The Full Moon is the most powerful one to work with, as it is the climax to the Moon's cycle.

Find a time when you can sit alone and be undisturbed, either inside or out, it is up to you.

Light the candles and drop the rose petals into the bowl of water together with some drops of the jasmine oil. The beautiful aroma of jasmine should make you remember what it is like to be loved and cherished.

Then take the rose quartz and place it in your left hand. This will help you to connect with your spiritual self. Just think happy thoughts and give thanks for what you have found. Do this for about 15 minutes. There is no rush. This will let the universe know how pleased you really are.

Leave the rose petals and oil until the next Full Moon. This will keep the love empowered and activated.

---*---

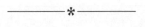

FINDING COMMON GROUND

A very important aspect in the growth of any relationship is that you get on with each other. Not in a physical way, which we will come to in the next chapter, but emotionally and spiritually. Emotionally, your partner must be able to understand all your personality traits – or flaws. For example you may dislike being too open, especially in front of his friends. He needs to gauge what is or isn't OK for you. Spiritually, does he know where you are coming from? And do you know where he is coming from? Men are very different from women in many respects. A good way to expand a relationship is to find common interests.

The following ritual is one that an American friend taught me. It includes a questionnaire, which is certainly a different approach for me. A lady once came to me for a reading and told me about a great guy she had met on holiday. The romance had continued afterwards but she was concerned because they didn't have much in common. He was a diving instructor and she was a nurse. As usual I had a ritual up my sleeve and I gave her this one. I told her that I would appreciate her telling me if it worked. She sent me an e-mail five months later to say it had helped them explore things they were both interested in and that this had helped to strengthen the bond between them. Why not try it yourself?

———*———

Developing Common Interests

You will need:
* Pink candle
* Rose incense

For this I want you to sit down and relax with your new love. You want to make this as simple as possible. Light the pink candle and have some rose incense burning. This will help you both to feel relaxed and able to think clearly. You want to call up your intuition to discover what your common interests are. Your intuition will also help you to develop some, even if you find at the beginning they are thin on the ground.

Just sit quietly and both close your eyes and think of your intuition as a rosebud opening as the sun shines. (I am trying not to make it too freaky or your boyfriend will be put off!) Then both open your eyes, and you will both be charged up with psychic energy. Now both answer these questions – and remember, be honest.

Question	You	Him
1. Do you have the same tastes in:		
Music		
Television programmes		
Food and drink		
Travel		
Books		
Newspapers		

Question	You	Him
2. Do you have the same leisure interests in: Sport The arts Dining Pubs/clubs Hobbies Nature walks/hill walking Travel and culture		
3. Do you have similar political views?		
4. Body clock wise, are you similar? Does he like late nights? Are you early to bed?		
5. A great gauge to see if you are both on the same wavelength – do you have the same sense of humour?		
6. Do you have similar moods/temperaments?		

These questions and answers will give you insight into how compatible you really are. Remember that opposites attract, so if you are belle of the ball and he melts into the background, that is OK. You can complement each other. Anyone who knows Ronald and me will know that we can be a very fiery couple and the reason we have arguments is because on many levels we are very different. But this is why our relationship is never boring!

Once you have completed your questionnaire, sit together holding hands. Close your eyes and imagine that you are sitting on thrones overseeing a brilliant kingdom. You both work together to keep it thriving, as you do with your relationship.

End the ritual by blowing out the candle together and give thanks for the help that you have received with this questionnaire from your Higher Self.

———— * ————

FINDING COMMON INTERESTS

Doing the above questionnaire and ritual will highlight what makes you tick as individuals and as a couple. If you find you do not have a lot in common, here's a list of things you could do together:

Salsa classes These are great, as you get to be physically close to one another and the music is so sexy.

Going to the cinema, art galleries and museums A bit of culture always helps to broaden your horizons and gives you more to talk about.

Sports, the gym, running or walking Get fit as well as get to know each other.

Join a sports club or operatic society These clubs help you to expand your social circle and keep your interests flowing.

It is up to you what common interests you take up, but whatever they are, they can really help the relationship gel.

LEARNING TO FEEL CLOSE TO EACH OTHER

You are entering a new part of the relationship which is known psychically as its 'summer'. Whether it is summer or not is not important – it is the season of the spirit of your relationship with each other. Summer is a powerful time when the masculine energies of strength, virility and hunting are at their most acute. Male and female energies working towards a common aim are most active at this time in the relationship. The purpose at this stage in your relationship is to be happy and peaceful.

You now need to set up a summer altar in your home, which will signify the growing energies between you and will honour the richness and wholeness of that time of year in your relationship. It will be the focus of your growing, expanding and of course loving relationship.

———— * ————

Building Your Summer of Love Altar

You and your boyfriend need to go for a long walk. It could be absolutely anywhere as long as you are among the sheer awesome brilliance of nature. Your aim is to connect with Mother Earth herself, the wise woman of the Earth.

You will walk together, hopefully arm in arm or hand in hand. Allow yourself to be guided by your own inner goddess, that brilliant spiritual being with great female power. Make no plans about where you are going, just allow yourselves to be guided.

What do you see? Are there any birds or animals around you? These are all symbols of your love. What types of tree and other plant are there? Fir trees, birch, grass, apple trees or even fern? Make a mental note of everything you see or, better still, have a notebook and pen handy. Also, collect little mementoes of this special time such as feathers, pebbles, stones, leaves – whatever feels right, just take it with you for your love altar.

Can you hear anything on your walk? Are the birds singing? Can you hear the snapping of twigs as you walk through a wood or the whoosh of waves battering on a beach? It is all telling you something. Are you listening? Make a note of what you hear.

Once your journey comes to its conclusion – you will intuitively know when this is – kiss your boyfriend and thank your inner goddess for the help she has given you today.

Now you need to build your love altar.

You will need:

* Green cloth
* 2 green candles
* 2 silver-coloured candlesticks
* 2 aventurine crystals
* Mementoes from your nature walk
* Happy photo of you both
* Rose incense

You will probably already have a love altar which you prepared to help you in your search for love. You can put that one away now. It has served its purpose. You have found love and want to build on it and develop the relationship. Give thanks for the help your altar has given you. You can now dismantle it. You can either keep its contents as a memento of this time or you can just discard all of it.

This time use a green cloth for the altar and green candles. Green is the colour associated with Mother Nature. You want her on your side here and this will help to connect with her. Put the two candles on either side of the altar. Beside these put the green aventurine crystals, which will help harness the positive energies of your love. In the middle place the happy photo of the two of you surrounded by the mementoes of the walk. The photo represents you both and the mementoes reveal the depth of your feelings for each other. They also reveal the hidden messages and spirituality of your love for one another.

You should both sit quietly at your altar for a while. Finally light the candles and incense. Just think about your relationship and how you want it to grow and develop.

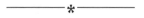

This is a lovely ritual and it really does ground the relationship and bring you closer together. I do this at least three times a year with my husband and I find it helps to clarify what I want out of my relationship. Ronald always tells me that the nature walk helps him to relax and focus on things going on in his life and also the relationship.

MESSAGES FROM YOUR NATURE WALK

On your nature walk your inner goddess and Mother Nature will both have been connecting with you as a couple. What were they trying to tell you? Here are the hidden meanings of the sounds, flowers, birds and animals you may have come into contact with on your walk.

Sounds

The sea This relates to your subconscious feelings.

The snap underfoot of branches This helps you to feel vibrations of love.

The crunch of sand Sand has a healing noise when it is stepped on. It helps you to accept the past and look forward to the future.

The pitter-patter of rain This signifies a time for reflection in your relationship.

There are many more that you can think about yourself.

Flowers and Other Small Plants

Apple blossom Your lover has a great inner beauty.

Aster Think carefully about your relationship.

Bluebell You are both over the disappointments of the past.

Bracken You are enchanted with each other.

Bramble Letting down your barriers will bring rewards.

Buttercup You are a beautiful being of light.

Cherry blossom Your relationship is still ripe.

Clover Your faith in each other may be tested soon.

Daffodil You both need to be honest about your feelings.

Daisy Eat, drink and be merry.

Dandelion Your love will conquer all.

Evening primrose You each adore the ground the other walks on.

Ferns Your love will stand the test of time.

Foxglove Are you listening to each other?

Heather You are both headstrong but have common aims.

Honeysuckle You are committed to each other.

Ivy Family matters will not tear you apart.

Tulip Your love will take some work, but it is worth it.

Wild grass Make sure that you have accepted that the past cannot be changed.

Wild rose Your love is free and growing.

Yarrow You will be blessed with a protective angel all your life.

Trees

Apple Your love will bear great fruit.

Beech An important letter is winging its way to you.

Birch Your love will need to grow at a slow rate.

Elder The tree of Venus, very lucky – good things will come.

Fir Outside influences could result in problems.

Hazel A wise elder is trying to give you advice, so listen.

Holly Your domestic situation will bring you happiness.

Oak You both have the wisdom to make the relationship work.

Pine Take your time, there is no need to rush.

Sycamore The relationship will be a growing experience and you will gain in wisdom.

Birds

Blackbird Listen to your inner voice.

Cock To hear one crow brings great luck and fertility.

Hen You're made for each other.

Crow Change is just ahead.

Cuckoo Prosperity is coming to you very soon.

Duck Your sorrow has gone and happiness will reign.

Eagle Very lucky – you have found your real soul mate.

Goose Trouble may come in the form of a person from the past.

Gull Storms ahead, so be ready.

Jackdaw Listen to your heart and not idle rumour.

Kingfisher Your union will be good for your health and well-being.

Magpie Be warned, as someone is trying to damage your love.

Owl Listen to the wisdom of an older person.

Peacock Luck is smiling on both of you.

Pigeon You will be married within two years and the bride will wear white.

Robin You will soon be thinking of living with each other.

Sparrow Happiness is with who you walk with today.

Swallow You will hear of a pregnancy very, very soon.

Woodpecker You will soon get rewards for your efforts.

Animals

Ant You will travel far and wide with the object of your affection.

Bat Your insecurities are unfounded and you need to be more assured.

Domestic dog A faithful friend will provide help in your relationship.

Domestic cat Your relationship needs communication to help it survive.

Fish A symbol of the ancient love goddess – your love is blessed.

Frog or Toad Many good things will come from your relationship.

Goat Your relationship will be hard work from start to finish.

Hare You know what your feelings are, so be honest.

Hedgehog You are both on the same wavelength.

Horse Things need to be taken slowly so you don't miss anything out.

Mouse There could be danger ahead, so be careful in your everyday life.

Sheep You will always mother this person.

Squirrel A message of hope is on its way.

So, what message did you get from your nature walk?

As I said, I do this walk at least three times a year just to help my husband and I see where we are heading in our relationship. A couple of years ago we did it as usual in a park called Chatelherault near to where we live in Hamilton. It has the most beautiful woodland and I like to just walk through the trees to see what vibes I get. As we were doing the walk a little black and white cat came out of nowhere and ran straight up to Ronald. He patted it, then it went off. Right away I said, 'We need to communicate more,' and it was true we had been not talking as much as usual. You may be surprised by the messages that come up from the walk, but take heed of them as they all make sense in the end.

MAINTAINING YOUR RELATIONSHIP

Maintaining a relationship is hard work. I know through my relationship with my husband that this is sooooooo true! How do you keep it exciting and fresh? Is there a special recipe to keep the romance alive? In this section I want to show you ways of maintaining your relationship with rituals, spells and exercises to give you that bit of extra psychic help.

There are four things to consider when you want to keep a relationship alive: romance, friendship, communication and staleness. All four must be addressed to make your relationship work. Let's look at how we can achieve that using our psychic abilities and rituals.

ROMANCE

Now, what *is* romance? Do you have any idea? How are we supposed to experience it if we don't know what it is? Romance to me is when Ronald bought me a pair of diamond earrings for my 32nd birthday. I was totally taken by surprise. Romance is often unexpected. Don't get me wrong: it doesn't have to be an expensive gift like my earrings. It can be a simple walk on the beach or holding hands in a park. You will recognise it because it makes you feel all warm and gooey inside. Romance is not something which should occur at special times of the year. It should happen at any moment to keep the relationship on its toes.

The following ritual is a lovely one which I often do

with Ronald just to revitalise the romantic side of our relationship. It also gives you some time just to enjoy each other's company. I discovered it while on my travels to southern Turkey. I was meditating under an olive tree when a lady in her fifties came to sit beside me. We spoke at length about what I did and why I was travelling around Turkey, which was to soak up the unique culture my father always spoke about. Then Ronald came to tell me my dinner was ready and the lady commented how much in love we looked. She told me about this ritual so that our love would remain strong throughout our lives. Which it has.

Romance Ritual

You will need:
* 1 pink candle
* 2 red pens
* 2 pieces of parchment paper
* Rose incense
* Pink ribbon
* 1 piece of rose quartz
* 1 piece of lapis lazuli

This should be performed at a Full Moon, as this will make your romance more acute. It needs time and space for it to work properly, so make sure you will not be disturbed. I have done it twice on trips away with Ronald just because I knew I could get the peace to do it then.

First I want you and your loved one to just sit and drink some wine – preferably with some bubbles in it. Just relax and talk about your love for each other.

Then, when you feel relaxed and ready, light your pink candle and use it to light your incense. The colour pink is important here as it signifies pure love and romance. It is the same for the rose incense, which also connects with Aphrodite, the goddess of love and romance.

Place the crystals next to each other, as the rose quartz represents the female power and lapis lazuli the male power. Putting these two energies together signifies you as a couple.

Now each of you should take a peace of parchment paper and use a red pen to write an affirmation of your love. Think about all the romantic times that you have had as a couple, then let the words flow from your pen. Put down on paper what you feel for this special person. Your partner will do the same so it is a beautiful binding moment.

Here is an example of an affirmation I once wrote for Ronald:

> 'You are my strong pillar,
> Helping to keep me upright and alive.
> You are my source of inspiration in all that I do.'

This is what he wrote for me:

> 'You are my snookums, my little bunny.
> You make my life sunny.'

Don't laugh! I know that it is very soppy, but it was written with feeling and love, which is the whole point of the exercise. It doesn't have to be Booker Prize material. If it comes from the heart then it will be fine. The idea is to have words which reflect your romance, so it is totally up to you what you write.

Once you have finished your affirmations, take the pink ribbon and cut it into two. Tie a piece around each of your parchments and finish it off with a bow. The pink ribbon and bow will seal the feelings behind the words, keeping them from harm or negative energies.

Then each month, week, year, whatever suits you both, go back and reaffirm what you said at the ritual.

————*————

So now that we know what romance is, what's next? Oh yes, now for friendship.

FRIENDSHIP

I make no apology for calling Ronald my best friend. Let's face it, I have known him now for 17 years. We have grown up together and shared good and bad times. I don't think that it is possible to have a loving and contented relationship without viewing your partner as a friend. A deep friendship will secure your love. It is built on trust, respect and mutual understanding.

To remind me of my friendship with Ronald and to remind him of his friendship with me we both have a very simple friendship bracelet which we wear all the time. It is something that I made with my own fair hands. It is a circle, which equals an unbreakable bond, a friendship which will live through good times and bad. Here is how you can make one for yourself and your special friend.

———————*———————

How to Make a Friendship Bracelet

You will need:
* 1 blue string
* 1 red string
* 1 green string
(You can get the proper string or cord from an art store.)

I made a really simple bracelet, but you can make more intricate ones if you want. Make the three pieces of string long enough to wrap around your friend's wrist. Then tie a knot in it in at the end. Plait the string and secure it at the end.

Next get your partner to make exactly the same type of bracelet for you.

Once you have both finished, get him to tie the one that he made for you around your wrist and then tie the one you made for him around his wrist.

When you are both wearing the bracelets you can sit quietly together and give thanks for your special friendship. Then perhaps do what Ronald and I do – hit the pub for a well-deserved drink and chat with friends. You have sealed your friendship and the bracelets symbolise it.

———————*———————

COMMUNICATION

This is a real biggy! Without communication a relationship will fail on many different levels. I would say that communication is the lifeblood of a relationship. I can't stress enough how important it is for keeping you together.

To make matters more difficult, women and men communicate in different ways. Women will tend to use codes and skirt around issues, hoping their man will understand what they are on about, whereas when men communicate it will normally be short and very much to the point. I know this is true, as Ronald says what he means and everything is so clear cut, while I will often expect him to get the whole story from my very sketchy information. Unsurprisingly, he normally doesn't have a clue and we waste time and energy talking at cross-purposes. So, I have learned to communicate clearly in my marriage.

A typical example of men and women getting their wires crossed comes from a very good friend of mine. Instead of asking her husband to go out with her for a meal on a Saturday night, she will tell him that she is feeling stressed and stir crazy. He might not understand that this means she needs a night out. By the time he gets the message the restaurants are fully booked and the night is ruined. I am sure that sounds familiar. At times like this your intuition can really help you out. It can help you understand what is really happening in the relationship and what the other person is trying to say.

The other aspect which can affect communication is spending valuable time together. If you don't do this, then it can be very difficult for communication to prosper.

As I mentioned earlier, I get so many letters from people who just can't communicate. I once had a letter from a woman who in 15 long years of marriage had never told her husband that sexual intercourse was painful. She just shut it all out and couldn't tell him how she was feeling.

By communication I don't just mean words, though, but also non-verbal communication. You can show your loved one that you care with cuddles, a peck on the cheek or a hug. These actions all speak volumes.

With a view to increasing communication I want to look at the Native Americans. They are incredibly wise and in the past used a whole range of methods of communication. Normally they took their inspiration from the nature around them. They burned wood to make smoke signals and had pow wows, group talks which allowed the tribe to discuss issues in a calm and peaceful way. Communication was the key to their strength.

When my sister Ayfer came back from her travels in America she told me about the Native Americans she had met and their wonderful stories and wisdom. She had spent some time living on a reservation and she told me that if there were disagreements or differing opinions on any subject then the talking pole or stick would be used. This was a special wooden pole, artistically decorated. When there was a pow wow the person holding the pole would be allowed to speak. Ayfer saw couples using it to resolve problems and discuss decisions they had to make.

When Ayfer came home and told me all about it I thought that this was a marvellous idea. What great wisdom we could learn from this sensitive culture. I use the talking pole now within family situations and when Ronald and I are having a disagreement. It is very simple and yet so effective. Here is how to do it.

————— * —————

Making a Talking Pole

You will need:
* Orange card
* Paints or pens (any colour you like)
* Paintbrushes
* Gold ribbon

You can do the first part of this ritual on your own. Take the orange card and sit with it in front of you. Allow yourself to think about the communication in your relationship. How do you talk to each other? Does it come naturally or do you really have to try hard to make it work? What about non-verbal communication – kissing and cuddling or holding hands and making eye contact? All of these point to a good stable relationship. Think about all the times you have cuddled up on the sofa to watch your favourite film.

Get in the 'communication zone'. Concentrate on the communication in your relationship and see what colours, shapes, symbols and words pop into your mind. Make a note of these, as you will need them later. Allow your mind to wander. This should take at least 10 minutes, so take your time. You are connecting with your psychic energy, letting it guide you on the design of your talking stick.

Once you have all your ideas down on paper, you can begin to design your talking stick. Take the orange card and use the pens and paints to write or draw the words and images that come to you. Your intuition is guiding you here. The card will have your own personal stamp on it and your energy will help it to work.

When you have finished your creative design, let the paint and ink dry. There is nothing worse than taking the time to create a beautiful object only to ruin it shortly afterwards. Remember not to rush this, just take your time.

Once your design is dry, roll up the card so that it forms a stick or pole and secure it using the gold ribbon. Gold is the colour which reflects the power of the Sun's rays. It will help the talking stick to exert a powerful positive power on your communication.

Now sit down with your loved one, hold the talking stick in all its glory and quietly say:

> *'Talking stick, help us to understand and love one another and give each other the time to express our feelings and our thoughts.'*

Your talking stick is now ready to use.

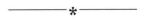

You can use your talking stick in two ways. The first is to use it anytime you have a problem that either of you wants to talk about. Once you are ready, whoever wants to talk must pick up the talking stick. The rules are that the person who has the stick must be allowed to talk uninterrupted. The person without the stick must listen. Once both of you have said your piece, it is time to cuddle. You will find this is a great way of getting your point across and resolving any conflicts you may have.

The second way to use the talking stick is when you have an argument or decision you can't agree on. Use the talking stick as before, then once you have made your decision, burn the stick. This represents the problem being resolved.

I have used the talking stick on many occasions, as I tend to be quite a fiery person who doesn't allow anyone else to say what they want. When I was deciding whether to have another child I used the talking stick with Ronald and it gave us both the space to say how we felt. Ronald loves using it, as it empowers him to speak.

STALENESS

A relationship going stale can be one of the things you can face if you stop making an effort. Letters I receive and clients I have seen point to the fact that this can become a reality for many relationships. Personally, I don't think that I have ever felt bored with Ronald. I truly don't think I have ever had the time to be. Ronald has a very dry sense of humour. He is calm by nature and often takes a pessimistic view. I am optimistic, usually hyper and sometimes need to be scraped off the ceiling. My head is often in the clouds with big ideas and dreams. Ronald helps to keep my feet firmly on the ground. As I mentioned earlier, we also enjoy some real ding-dongs. We just never have a boring minute. But not all couples are as lucky as we have been. Being unable to break from routine or getting into predictable habits could mean that your relationship is on a crash course to failure. How do you keep the excitement alive? And the laughter and fun?

Now I have already made it clear how important it is to be physically and spiritually cleansed. It prepares you for a variety of things, including love to grow in your life. What I am going to ask you to do now will help to bring back the excitement in your relationship. It will also allow positive energies to increase between you, which in turn will increase the interest and excitement. You are both going to learn to connect with your inner god and goddess. It may sound strange, but you have just got to trust me on this one. I know that it works.

Putting the Fizz Back in Your Relationship

You will need:
* Rose oil
* Lavender oil
* Rose petals
* Lavender flowers
* Rose-scented soap
* Lavender body lotion
* Orange-scented lotion
* Bath
* Wine
* 2 silver or pewter goblets
* Game such as Scrabble, Twister, Monopoly or Cluedo

I want you to start by sharing a bath with your lover. It is important to do this together as it is part of the ritual that both of your spirits are cleansed at the same time. I don't want to hear excuses that your bath is too small – my husband and I are far from petite and we manage just fine.

When running the bath, put in a couple of drops of rose oil

and lavender oil. Also, if you can get them, lavender flowers and rose petals. Let the bath sit for five minutes so that the essence of the flowers infuses in the water.

Now both of you get into the bath. Relax in the water and sense that your spirits are being cleansed together. You will connect with your loving energies and this will help you get a sense of what you felt when the relationship was just beginning. The lavender oil and flowers will calm your mind, body and spirit. The rose oil and petals will allow love to shine through. Rose has a high vibrational energy which helps the heart to open and fill with love. Cleanse each other with rose-scented soap.

After the bath, dry each other and use lavender body lotion on yourself and orange-scented lotion on your lover. Lavender will relax you and awaken the goddess that lies within you. Orange lotion will awaken the god that lies within him.

Put on loose clothing or a robe, sit together and ask your inner god and goddess to help you to keep a spark in your relationship. Celebrate their help by having a glass of wine each in a silver or pewter goblet. This relates to the Moon and helps the emotional side of your relationship.

Then play a game such as Scrabble, Monopoly or Cluedo. This will help you to connect with each other on a spiritual and intellectual level. You don't even have to have a board game. Twister is great fun. Ronald and I often play treasure hunt – we hide objects from each other and take it in turns to look for them while the other person is saying 'hot' or 'cold'. With childish play like this the worries of the world are left behind and you have your own special space and time with each other.

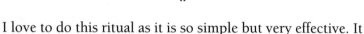

I love to do this ritual as it is so simple but very effective. It will make you feel more interested in each other. Your lives will be full of fun and your relationship will be too.

This chapter has been great, hasn't it? We have looked at how you can take your relationship forward from the first date and then develop it. A relationship is like a living organism which needs food to help it grow. I hope that you have enjoyed my novel and unique approach to doing this. Now on to another fun subject – sex!

Chapter 6
SEX AND SEXUALITY

THIS CHAPTER IS PROBABLY the most difficult for me to write. The main reason – and I am being totally honest here, guys – is that I am a bit of a prude. And me a psychosexual counsellor as well! I am not a prude under the covers, as my husband will testify, but talking about the whole subject gets me blushing. But for all my loyal fans I will get over my embarrassment and help you find the love goddess that lies within you and become a woman with sexuality oozing out of every pore.

By now I would be hoping that you have met someone who is special to you, a twin soul, a soul you can be free with and love with all your heart. When you are with him you feel safe and secure. You just look at him and your legs turn to jelly. You are able to talk freely to him about your passions and desires. All of the hard work we have put in will now be worthwhile. Your relationship will be sealed through passionate sex.

I am certainly not here to preach to you and tell you when sex should occur. You should listen to your own heart, mind and body. If it feels right for you, then it is OK. Feeling positive about yourself will also help you decide what is right for you. Feeling safe with a man – at least knowing him – is a good start to a healthy and fulfilling sex life. In this chapter I want to show you practical rituals and ceremonies you can use to connect with your female vital force, or as I like to call it, your FVF.

PREPARATION

When two lovers come together in sexual union it is a powerful expression of life force. You can prepare your body, mind and soul for this special union.

BODY

Your body expresses your desires. When you meet your lover your heart will beat faster, your breathing will increase and your pupils will dilate. Your body is a temple and it needs energy to function. Eat plenty of fruits and vegetables. Try and maintain an organic diet as far as possible. Drink plenty of water to flush out toxins. Purify yourself.

During sex your body expresses so many levels of your being. You must feel comfortable in it. Look at yourself in a mirror and tell yourself: 'I am a beautiful being of light.' Believe how special you are. Remind yourself of my confidence-busting exercises (*see pages 33–36*).

Your body expresses how you feel, so prepare it by dancing to your favourite music. Go on, get your fave CD or album out and put it on. Crank it up and feel the music take you away. Just let yourself go. Do it when no one else is in your home and just let rip. Remember to close your curtains or blinds so that the neighbours don't think you have gone mad. Just enjoy the feeling of liberation that it gives you. I enjoy salsa music or Turkish traditional music and as an avid belly dancer with the belly for it I use it to loosen myself up. You can use whatever is comfortable. Dancing helps you to listen to your body's needs and to react to them.

Once you know your body and can listen to it, the next stage in the process is being able to act on your feelings.

Touch is such an important aspect of showing affection and love. If you want to be touched, then ask your partner to do so. The best way to start this is by massage, which I will discuss further later. Or, when you feel insecure, down or just in need of support, ask for a hug. Hugs and cuddles don't cost a penny and they make you feel great – you feel a warm glow inside. This is especially true for me when Ronald or my children hug me. Hugging will help to bond your relationship and therefore it is very important.

MIND

Your mind is what you use every second of the day to make important decisions, to argue and reason. It tells you what is right and wrong, and it has the most amazing ability – the imagination. The imagination is where you can run wild and naked with your lover. I truly believe that great sex begins in the mind.

--------------*--------------

Mind Sex

I want you to sit comfortably. Close your eyes and become aware of your breathing. Listen to your breath as it gets slower and more controlled. Feel at peace.

Imagine you are with your lover. Make the setting all your own. It can be anywhere. Where would you go with your lover if expense, distance or time were not limiting factors? For example, I would love to be in a log cabin on a snow-covered mountain in Austria, all warm and cosy lying with my lover on a sheepskin rug in front of a roaring log fire. I can smell the fire and hear the crackle of the wood. The wind would be howling outside and the moon would light up the snow outside so it looked blue. I would feel safe and secure in the arms of my lover, who could be anyone from George Clooney to Brad Pit.

What is your romantic scenario? Imagine the scene. Imagine feeling safe and secure in the arms of your dream lover. Imagine what his touch feels like against your skin. What are the sights, sounds and smells around you? Let your imagination run wild . . . You are in control of it all.

--------------*--------------

This exercise will allow you to develop a picture of your real partner in your mind's eye just by closing your eyes. You can easily recall it at times when it is needed, for example if you want to get in the mood or if you are missing him. Training your mind helps it to function at its best for sex.

SOUL

There are many definitions of the soul. It is easily confused with the spirit, although they do mean different things. Both are part of us – they are our connections to the non-physical world, or spiritual plane. The spirit is the energy of the universe and you can think of it as our vital spark. The soul is, I believe, the very essence of our being. It is our intelligence. It connects us to the spiritual energy we use every second of every day. When you look at your lover and deep, deep down you just know that he is the one for you, that is your soul speaking to you.

To get your soul into shape for sexual contact with your loved one, there is nothing better than the power of a labyrinth. This is a symbol of the soul. It is a structure which can be built out of hedges, trees or stone, and it takes the shape of twists and turns that you walk around. There is normally one correct way to go from start to finish, with many dead ends in between. If you are lucky enough to live near a park, stately home or castle, you may have a labyrinth on your doorstep. I have one near to me in Chatelherault in Hamilton and I have often been there for inspiration and nourishment for my soul.

Don't worry if you don't live near a labyrinth, as you can build one in your very own back garden. All you need is a pile of small stones or pebbles. I have a friend who collected her pebbles from a beach near her home and she felt that collecting them this way meant they had the heal-ing power of the sea. Collect them on a nature walk with your lover, but make sure you take a bag, as your pockets won't be big enough. You want your labyrinth to be big enough to walk around – the size of a small garden will suffice.

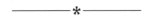

Creating Your Labyrinth

You will need:
* Pebbles or small stones

Sit in your back garden or a space that you have designated your special zone. It could be a park or a beach. Have your piles of stones or pebbles with you.

A simple labyrinth that I made out of pebbles from a beach in Arran.

Close your eyes and feel your intuition awakening. Hold some of the stones to feel their energy and allow Mother Nature to guide you in the shape you have to make. Your intuition will make sure that a shape pops into your head. Use this, but keep it simple and not too convoluted.

Once you have made your labyrinth, walk around it. As you follow it through, think about your lover. Imagine your souls connecting and how whole you will feel.

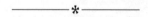

This is a lovely exercise to do and it certainly is food for the soul. I have a friend who did this when she felt uncertain whether the time was right to go to bed with her boyfriend. She constructed her labyrinth using just a stick and sand on a beach, which is another easy way of making one. She told me that once she had walked around the gentle curves of her labyrinth she saw that going to bed with her lover was the natural step to take. She said it was as if her soul had spoken to her. I like to explain it in the sense that going through the labyrinth is like finding your soul again.

A labyrinth is a very powerful symbol which will help you not only in your sexual relationship but also in your everyday life.

AWAKENING PASSION

Now that your body, mind and soul are prepared for love-making I want us to look at how to activate the passion in your life. The following rituals will enhance your sensitivity and improve your sexual experience. I want sex to be an immensely pleasurable experience.

The first ritual is a lovely one my grannie told me about. Her gran told her a story about two Romany lovers who felt their love life was not all it could be. The garland they made signified the eternal bond between them. Once they had displayed it on their caravan, the Sun shone and love never left them. Ah, what a lovely story. Yours can be too.

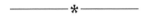

Garland for Lovers

You will need:
* Branches with leaves
* Red and white flowers
* Red berries
* Garden wire
* Yarn

Now don't look at this and say, 'Oh no, too technical,' because it is easy. A garland is easy to make and is a beautiful symbol of your love. It is a great way to herald the next stage of your relationship.

The first thing you need to do is to take note of what season you are in. Then work out what flowers and berries will be available. For example, if you were making your garland in summer you could use roses and the berries could be raspberries. The flowers and berries represent passion and fertility.

Go out to the woods or local park and collect your

branches, leaves and flowers. Let your intuition guide you. This is a great grounding exercise to help the ritual do its work. If you collect leaves and branches from a tree, then say thank you to her. She is giving you a part of herself and it is only polite to give thanks.

If you can't find the branches, leaves and flowers you have chosen, then just get the ones which are in season at a florist. Florists are a great source of information about flowers, so ask them what would be appropriate.

As you are gathering the greenery for your garland, no matter how, turn your thoughts to your loved one. Sense him near to you throughout this meaningful ritual. You will feel guided doing this and it will be your own inner goddess who will be helping you find the right things to symbolise your special love.

When you get home, settle yourself down. Think about the unique bond you have with your partner. Then set to work. Take the garden wire and bend it into the shape of a circle. How big you make it will depend on you, but in general the size of a steering wheel will suffice. Then wrap the ends together so that the circle is secure.

Take your branches with the leaves and one by one weave them around the circumference of the wire. If you feel that they won't stay in place, use yarn or wool to tie them to the wire. Continue until you end up with a circle full of greenery. Then add the flowers and berries. You should be able to just pin them in using their stems. As you do this, think about the love you feel and how special it is. Take your time over it, as this can't be rushed.

Once you have finished, present your unique love garland to your partner. By custom you should leave it at the door and when it dries out you can use it as a wall hanging. It is a symbol of the wholeness you both feel as a couple and the circle is a powerful sign that your love will last for eternity.

*

My grannie was a florist, so she knew what she was talking about when she told me all about this. I made a garland for Ronald and I still have it to this day proudly displayed above my fireplace. When I look at it I think about all the good times I have had with Ronald and all the good times still to come. I am sure that when you do yours it will put your relationship into perspective.

HELP FROM YOUR INNER GODDESS

I spoke about your inner goddess at the beginning of the book. This is the time when you really need to connect with her. She will help you to enjoy all the fruits of your labour. She allows you to express those feelings and desires that you may find difficult or awkward. She is a helper and healer. She is there, you only have to know how to connect with her, and in all my years with Ronald she has never let me down. She keeps my feminine vital force in check.

The following ritual will help you to discover the beauty that your goddess can bring. I was told about it by my Scottish gran, who would often do it for friends and family. I am sure she did it for herself too, but she was a very modest lady who liked to keep personal matters to herself. This is such a beautiful ritual it puts a smile on my face and a glow in my heart just writing about it.

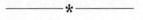

A Shrine to Your Sex Life

You will need:
* 2 white candles
* Frankincense incense
* An object to represent lovers (a photo of you both, a postcard of a painting signifying love or even a small ornament)
* White flowers in a red vase

First, go into all the rooms in your home. Choose a room that you feel relaxed and safe in, somewhere you can feel free and uninhibited. You need a surface to build a shrine which can be left alone and will not be disturbed. You can use the likes of a coffee table, windowsill or even the top of a CD rack, which is what I have used in the past. Well, it needs to be out of the way of children and pets!

The ritual should be carried out at a time when you can get peace and quiet to work your magic. Place the two white candles on your surface, one at either corner. They represent the coming together of two souls. White symbolises pure love. Then in the middle place the lovers' symbol and beside that the vase of flowers. The white flowers are for peace and stillness. They symbolise time standing still for you as lovers, so the moment of union lasts longer, and allows the relationship to stay focused. The lovers' object represents your boyfriend and yourself. The red vase shows that at the centre of all this love is a potent sexual power. In front of these place the incense safely in a holder. Frankincense is excellent for heightening your awareness and senses. Goddesses within the spiritual realm also favour it.

Sit comfortably and just slow down your mind. Close your eyes and slow your breathing. Breathe in through your nose and out through your mouth. Meditate for a couple of moments so that your mind becomes sharp and focused on the job in hand. You may find it easier to do this by imagining that as you breathe in through your nose your breath is made up of golden light and as you breathe out through your mouth the golden breath fills the room, bringing you a feeling of peace and love. A gold mist will cover the room and it will protect you and heal you during your ritual.

Now light the candles, then the incense. As you do this, ask your inner goddess to help you to acknowledge your twin soul and for your sexual chemistry to match. Imagine you are in the arms of your lover and that you feel safe, secure and cherished. The goddess within craves sexual union and you know that you are well matched. You can think about an intimate time you have had with your lover or, if it hasn't happened yet, fantasise about what it might be like. This ritual will help your goddess to respond to your needs. Just sit until it feels right to end the ritual.

I would suggest doing this once a month to help you activate the goddess's guidance in matters of love or, if you need help with difficulties, then do the ritual to call upon her.

A family member of mine did this ritual a couple of months after she had had a baby. She had had trouble with sex ever since she was five months pregnant. She just didn't feel sexy anymore and couldn't bear her husband touching her. Once she had done the ritual I couldn't believe the change in her. She seemed to glow and radiate. In fact we met for coffee and spent most of the time just giggling like a couple of schoolgirls. She couldn't believe how good the ritual had made her feel. She felt that her goddess had wings which shielded her and made her feel safe. She felt like a woman again, and sexy. At least her husband now had a big smile on his face and to this day he buys me a drink whenever he sees me. I am certain that you will enjoy all the sensations that will come after the ritual, too – just be ready for them.

GETTING IN THE MOOD FOR SEX

Sex is such an important part of a caring and loving relationship. But let's be honest, no matter how connected you are to your inner goddess, if you are tired and stressed you will find it hard to get in the mood for love. Sometimes when you are feeling low emotionally and physically, communication, both verbal and physical, just stops. The following is my guide to overcoming limiting factors and enjoying great sex.

TACKLING STRESS

Low libido in both men and women normally comes from general factors such as tiredness, stress, overwork, diet, alcohol and drug-taking. These all take their toll on your amorous feelings. If stress is your problem, as it is for so many of us, then you need to tackle it head on. Fortunately, there are simple strategies you can adopt to reduce your stress.

Organise Your Work

Get your workload sorted out. Learn to delegate and pass things on. Then prioritise all the tasks you have left. Take regular breaks during your day and have a cup of refreshing herbal tea or even take a walk to clear your head.

If you don't work from home, make it a work-free zone. If you have to bring work home, try to do it on the train before you get to your front door. If do you work from home, as I do, make sure you set clear boundaries for when you should be working and when you are not.

Childcare is my biggest stress. If your child is at school or nursery, make sure you have a back-up plan if they are sick or off school.

Get Assertive

So many people write to me completely stressed out because they just can't say no. So often we take on extra work or family duties just to please others. Next time you are asked to do something you have no time for, say no. Be firm and concise and you will find you feel elated at the feel-good factor this gives you.

Eat Well

Stimulants such as alcohol and caffeine have been found to aggravate stress levels and response. Sure they give you an initial high, but this soon wears off, leaving you tired and sluggish. Drink herbal teas or fruit infusions instead. If you don't like these, water or fruit juice will do the trick. Vitamin C has been found to help combat stress levels by reducing stress hormones found in the blood. Eating plenty of fresh fruits and vegetables will help you get the vitamin C you need.

Take Some Exercise

Exercise helps you not only to increase your energy levels but also to reduce stress. Make time for a little exercise every other day. For maximum benefit, the recommended time is 30 minutes. Do something you really enjoy and this will not feel like a chore. I enjoy walking, dancing to Latin American music and swimming; you decide what to put into your own routine. You will only benefit!

Once you have been able to deal with your stress you will feel better and more in control of your life.

GETTING THE REST YOU NEED

Make your bedroom a relaxing haven. It should only be used for sleep and relaxation, but if you must work in it, as I do, get a screen to hide your computer and other work equipment when you are not working. Choose relaxing colours for your room, such as lilac or cream, and have soft lighting.

Before going to bed don't eat anything too heavy, as this raises your metabolic rate and will cause a restless night's sleep. It is also best not to take coffee or tea before going to bed, as these stimulants can cause you to be too awake before bedtime. Instead you could have a milky drink or a herbal tea to settle you down for the night.

Another way to relax is to have a nice bath with aromatherapy oils or herbs. I make up a muslin pouch of dried lavender, camomile and a couple of drops of sandal-wood, then I just tie it up and pop it into my running bath to infuse. I always find this helps me to relax and become sleepy.

If you get the rest and sleep you need then you will be able to tackle your stress levels and this will allow you to manage your life effectively. If you are feeling in control then your sex life will improve, as you will have the time and energy for it.

APHRODISIACS

As for mood enhancers, the following is a range of foods you can eat to get you in the mood. I will also look at herbs that you can use.

Asparagus My mother swears by this. The vegetable not only has certain mood enhancers in its nutrients but also increases the mobility of sperm, so it is good for male fertility. My mum says that when she conceived my sister Soraya she had just had a plate of asparagus pasta my dad had made!

Chocolate Oh yes, chocolate was called the food of the gods by the Incas who discovered it. It has chemicals which act as stimulants and provide a feel good all over factor.

Chocolate has been known to give women orgasms just by eating it. Well, that is what my friend Helen told me, and she should know, she is a doctor.

Garlic OK, not great for the breath, but it does increase libido. Its effect can last for many hours and it seems to work well on men who have been feeling too tired for sex. It seems to give them the energy for it.

Honey Throughout history this has been noted for its sexual potency. In Turkey it is often used in wedding cake or treats to get you in the mood for love. It was even used in the Arabic world for growing males, as it was believed that it could make them bigger. Take it in tea or on toast.

Oats Oats have amazing healing properties and are good for the skin, making it soft and supple to the touch and therefore a turn on. A bath infused with steeped oats tied up in a muslin bag is great for the skin of the whole body. It also increases the blood supply to the sex organs, making them work more efficiently.

Herbs

This list of aphrodisiac herbs was kindly given to me by Helen Speed, who is a herbalist I often went to see in the past. As with all herbs, make sure you get the advice of a herbalist before taking them, as they can interact with medication you may be on.

For both sexes:

Ginger
Korean ginseng
Siberian ginseng

Ginkgo biloba
Gotu kola
Rhodiola
Rosea

For women only:

Celery seed
Chinese angelica

For men only:

Saw palmetto

These herbs work by influencing either the nervous system, thus improving mood, energy and sensory awareness, for example oats and rhodiola, the sex hormones, for example saw palmetto and celery seed, or the circulation to the sex organs, for example ginkgo, garlic and ginger. Some herbs have a combination of these actions, for example ginseng and gotu kola.

In most of her 81 years on this planet my Scottish gran used herbal lotions and potions for all sorts of things. She often made up herbal potions for newly married brides and I am sure a lot of it was to help them in their sex lives.

If you have eaten all the honey you can and given the herbs a try, then you could use my very own tried and tested love potion. This is a variation on one passed down by my Turkish family and I have seen it working many times. It will stir your loins and help you to harness your potent sexual power. If you are feeling nervous about sex with your loved one or if you have not been feeling like sex, why not give it a try? I am 100 per cent sure it will work for you.

Ruth's Love Juice

You will need:
* Bottle of medium dry white wine
* ¼ teaspoonful of brown organic sugar
* Fresh sweet basil
* 1 teaspoonful of Australian honey (for preference, as Australian is the most potent, but any will do)
* Ceramic jug

Make your love juice on a night when there is a Full Moon. This will give the potion the maximum sexual energy.

Take the wine and pour it into the jug. Then add the brown sugar, which represents love, and basil, for commitment. Then add the honey, as it is an aphrodisiac. Stir the liquid with a wooden spoon. Then place it in your fridge to chill it.

At night, when you have your lover at home with you, take the potion out of the fridge. Don't forget to strain it so that you don't get a big mouthful of basil. Toast your relationship, saying, 'Cheers. May love alight for us tonight.' Take a drink and then see the passion ignite.

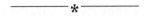

This has worked on every person who has used it and I have given the recipe to many hundreds of people.

CREATE YOUR OWN INNER SANCTUARY

Take a look at your bedroom. Does it look like a place that welcomes the act of love or is it full of clutter and not very welcoming? Creating the right environment for love can make all the difference to your mood.

To begin with, make sure that you have control of your clutter. Clutter can be defined as anything in and around your living space that you have no need for. It can be a shoebox, a pile of magazines from years ago or pot pourri that hasn't had an aroma in months. Put your clutter away in boxes and if you don't need it, then toss it. I am telling you, you will feel better for it. Clutter can make a relationship stagnate and your love life slow and uninteresting.

The colour of love-making and passion is red, so if you can incorporate a splash of this colour in your bedroom, so much the better. Red has a high vibration, so it can lift the senses and help you to get in the mood for love.

Look at your room and make sure that it is balanced. For example, ensure your pillows match in colour and quantity and that you have two lamps, one at either side of the bed, or two pictures. Having even numbers of things, symmetry and pairs will all help to create a room which welcomes love. Pairs and matched objects symbolise togetherness and sexual energy.

Also, make sure your room is nice and welcoming with warm and cosy textiles and fabrics. They should be pleasurable to touch and give a sense of warmth and care.

Scent is also an important factor, as it activates the sexual hormones of both sexes. I suggest you have a ceramic oil burner in your room and burn essential oils such as ylang ylang, sandalwood and jasmine, which are all known for their aphrodisiac properties. If you wish, you can use the corresponding incenses of ylang ylang, sandalwood and jasmine.

With all this, your room will become an inner sanctuary where you and your lover can relax and let your passion run riot. You will also discover that your mood is lifted to a higher spiritual level.

'TOUCH FEELY GETS YOU IN THE MOODY'

The gift of touch is in essence the most basic way in which you can connect with your partner. Not only does it help you to feel close to your partner, but it also strengthens the bond between you.

As you know, I am half Turkish and all my life it has never failed to amaze me just how into touch the Turks are. They hold hands, cuddle and kiss at the drop of a hat. We could learn a lot from them in our more reserved society. In Turkey massage has also been a way of life for many since they were young. There are many *hamams* or Turkish baths where you can steam yourself silly, swim and then get a big muscular masseuse to give you a good going over.

I had a Turkish friend called Atilla who gave me the following recipe for a love massage. It is sure to blow your lover's mind! The oils will help both of you to relax and become aware of all the positive aspects of your relationship, especially in the area of sex. This is also great if you have been feeling low or your lover's libido has not been on form. It will heighten the senses ready for a night of sheer delight. Atilla assured me that he had used it many times on brides or bridegrooms just before their big day, as it is the custom in Turkey to get a good wash and massage at that time. He told me that many came back to tell him of their sexploits on honeymoon. I can even vouch for it myself, but that is all I am revealing. Just try it yourself.

———————*———————

Atilla's Love Massage

You will need:
* Small plate or saucer
* Small plastic funnel
* 25 ml (¾ fl oz) brown glass bottle (available from chemists)
* 5 drops patchouli oil
* 5 drops sandalwood oil
* 2 drops ylang ylang oil
* 1 drop tangerine oil
* 20 ml (just under ¾ fl oz) grapeseed oil or any other carrier oil

Take the glass bottle and add the grapeseed oil to it. A small plastic funnel will make this easier. Then add 5 drops of patchouli oil, 5 drops of sandalwood oil, 2 drops of ylang ylang oil and 1 drop of tangerine oil.

Once you are ready, get your partner to lie comfortably, either on the bed or on the floor. It is also important that the room is warm, as you don't want goosebumps getting in the way of your fun. Take the bottle of oil, turn it around three times clockwise on the palm of your hand and say:

'These oils will find our passions stirred with the touch of our hands and the aroma of love.'

Then pour some oil onto a saucer and take some of it between your palms and fingers. Rub it into your hands so that they are warm as they touch your lover's body. There is nothing worse than lying back and trying to feel sexy only to get a shock when cold hands touch you.

It is now time for you to start the massage. Make sure that you are comfortable, relaxed and in a position where you won't strain your back. I would suggest you start with your lover's back and work your way around, letting your imagination run wild. It is up to you what you do, but remember that massaging erogenous zones is fun and can help your passion develop. The intimacy which comes with the sense of touch is very erotic.

After you have had the pleasure of massaging your lover, let him return the favour. I am sure that this will only help your love life and overall relationship.

So, how was it for you? The rituals and wisdom given here will help you bond in an intimate and magnificent way and your heightened sexual experience will bring you so much closer. You are on a journey that has just got a whole lot more exciting.

Chapter 7
RUTH THE TRUTH'S LOVE ORACLE

THIS FOR ME IS THE most exciting of my seven chapters, as it will answer so many questions you have about your love life. I developed it myself, but it is based on an old oracle which was found in the ruins of a palace in southern Turkey. It was used to answer the deepest questions of royal families of the times. I have used it with people of all ages, sexes and backgrounds, from a consultant radiologist to a druid priestess. Everyone who has tried it has received a message that they could understand and enjoy. I am sure that you will have hours of fun with it, but as with all things I do there is a logical step-by-step approach to get the best out of it. So read on to discover how to use the oracle of love.

THE FIRST STEP

For the oracle to work the first thing you must do is to protect yourself from outside forces and influences. These may arise because you are about to partake in your own psychic awakening. So you must make sure that your spirit is kept safe from psychic attack. I have had this on only one occasion and it happened when I did a reading for a guy at a party without protecting myself first. I left myself open to his negative vibes and I felt ill for many days afterwards until my gran stepped in to help me clear my aura. To save you from ever having to do this I have devised a very simple exercise for you to protect yourself.

One of the most powerful ways to protect yourself during any psychic work is to introduce yourself to your guardian spirit. These spirits guard our own psychic pathways and gates – the gateways that link us to the psychic realm. Any person can have a whole variety of spirit guides working on their behalf at any time. You only have to work with one to do the oracle properly. If you know who your guardian spirit is, then you can call upon them any time you are doing psychic work.

————— * —————

Connecting with Your Guardian Spirit

Sit down and make yourself comfortable in a place where you know you will not be disturbed. Become aware of your surroundings, then relax. Turn your attention to your breathing. Breathe in slowly through your nose and out through your mouth. Allow any thoughts swimming about your head to just float away with each exhale of your breath. Just do this for a few moments so that you can become as relaxed as possible.

Once you know that you are relaxed in body, mind and spirit, turn your attention to your guardian spirit. Ask them to reveal themselves to you. At this point you may feel a draught at the back of your neck, a tingle on your head or even a soft reassuring pat on your shoulder. Do not be afraid, this is just your spirit telling you that they are there ready to protect you in a spiritual way.

You may actually get a mental image of your guardian spirit. When my Scottish gran did this for the first time as a young woman, her guardian angel was a young soldier called Tam from the First World War. His job was to look after my gran and he did this well all of her life. My guardian spirit is always an angel with the most glorious iridescent gold and white wings which shield me from anything negative.

Don't worry if you don't get a clear image or message right away – with time and practice, it will come. Just be reassured that your guardian spirit is there looking after your interests. Thank them for looking after you.

Then, when it feels right, imagine your feet have roots that hold you firmly in place. You are grounding yourself after this spiritual exercise.

Then imagine that a large bubble of golden light covers your whole body and protects you. You can see out, but no negative vibes can get in.

———————*———————

You are now ready for the next stage.

THE SECOND STEP

Now I want you to think about the issues in your love life. What do you want to discover from the oracle? Is there anything that is troubling you or that you are unsure about? Think about this just now. You will get an answer from the oracle – either a direct one or one which it feels will be important to you.

THE THIRD STEP

Finally, look at the oracle itself (*see page 190*). It is composed of a circle with 12 sections. Each section is ruled by a symbol and has six outcomes, as six is the number of love in numerology.

I want you to sit with the oracle in front of you. Keep thinking of your issues and questions.

Place the first finger of your right hand in the centre of the oracle and say:

'*Oracle, answer my query,
as I want my love life never to grow weary.*'

Close your eyes and run your right finger around the oracle. Feel guided as to where to stop. Immediately open your eyes and look at the symbol you have chosen, then the numbers one to six. Which number are you drawn to? This is your oracle number.

Now look up the symbol you chose and the number you picked and read your answer. It couldn't be simpler!

I'm sure you will have loads of fun with my love oracle. You can consult it whenever you have a question in

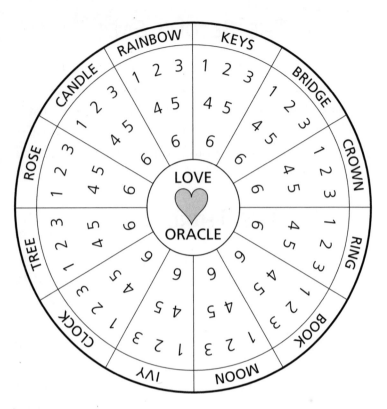

mind or when you want to see what your love life will involve next. Enjoy it.

KEYS

The symbol of the keys conveys that security and the ability to have control over a situation are important. It also concerns the opening up of emotions in your life. The importance of this cannot be underestimated.

1. You feel insecure in your relationship but have no real reason to. You must have more confidence in yourself. Personal development will help. Advice you read in a

book will really strike a chord with you – don't allow the message to pass you by.

2. Your fears that your lover could be looking at others may be correct. But he is worth fighting for, so don't give up. You have a role to play in all of this, so take some of the responsibility and stop burying your head in the sand.

3. Your lover is a free spirit who needs his space. You can't have control over him, but this is part of the attraction. Don't crowd him or you will be disappointed. You could learn a lot from him about how to relax into life, as you have been a little uptight of late, haven't you?

4. Your love life is blossoming. You deserve happiness and you have found it. Don't let the insecurities and let downs of past relationships waste what you have now. It is no time to feel insecure, as you will miss so much fun if you do, and life is for living and enjoying just now.

5. You are not settled in your love life at present and may be tempted by another's interest, but ask yourself whether it is worth it. The answer to this should be 'no', as what you have is very special. Love like this doesn't come around every day. Ask yourself why you are not settled and the answer will show you that there is something far deeper going on.

6. After a bumpy start your relationship will become more secure. However, the man you are with can be a bit of a control freak and you may have to learn to modify his behaviour. It won't be easy, but it can be done, so be patient and stay focused.

BRIDGE

A bridge symbolises transition from one set of circumstances in life to another. The road of change is not always easy and can be quite a challenge. There are many rewards to be gained, though, which will make the hard work worth it.

1. Your love life will improve once you make the decision to change an aspect of your current career. Go with your gut feeling, as it will help you make the right decision, one you won't regret. Study and qualifications are also highlighted here – these can only advance your career and your love life will benefit as a result.

2. A loved one will soon bring news of a change to his domestic situation. You won't feel relaxed about this and may worry about the consequences of his actions. The best way forward will be to be honest and upfront with him so that he realises that perhaps his views are blinkered.

3. Your love life is about to change as a friendship develops into a deeper love. This is what you both want and need, so go with it. Fate has allowed this situation to arise for a reason and you would be foolish not to take the help offered. Don't feel awkward, as the feelings are mutual.

4. Life never stands still – well, this is true certainly of yours. You will soon hear news from abroad that will make your day. You may have a decision to make of a romantic nature, but think about what is being offered and don't jump in without considering all the options

first. Whatever you decide, your life will never be the same again – which is a good thing.

5. News of a pregnancy will be of importance to you. It will be unplanned, but the initial shock will soon turn to joy and happiness. The baby will be a symbol of everlasting love and will be born into a happy relationship. Some things like this rock your whole world, but the ripple effect will only be positive in the long run.

6. Your lover has wild ideas, but they will become reality as long as you give him support and a shoulder to cry on at difficult times. You are his rock when his plans seem a million miles away from reality. With you by his side he will be successful beyond anyone's expectations.

CROWN

The regal crown represents reaching the pinnacle of everything you are doing in life. It reveals that you have the kingdom at your feet, but don't be too complacent, as it can all be taken away from you if you let your guard down, and with power comes great responsibility.

1. You have been in relationships in the past where you have had to carry the other person on a personal level, as he has had little get up and go or ambition and needed you to be there to make it all happen for him. Don't let history repeat itself, as you have enough on your plate without carrying passengers as well. You need a man who is independent and able to do things for himself.

2. You feel that the relationship you are in is too good to be

true, but just relax and enjoy it, as the person you have found is very special. He has real feelings for you, so don't jeopardise it by feeling insecure all the time. Show your feelings by giving him plenty of hugs and kisses. He enjoys affection, so give it to him in bundles.

3. You like the best things in life. Little luxuries are important to you and they make your life worthwhile. You can be very materialistic and the person you are with will never be able to give you the things you want. You need to be honest with him so that a decision about the future you both want and need can be reached.

4. You are a princess, but you haven't met your prince yet, just a lot of frogs along the way. Your prince will come very soon, though. He will be at a social event that has been organised by a very good friend of yours, so get out and party. Life will soon be great in your kingdom.

5. The person in your life finds responsibility very difficult to handle. It stems from a difficult family background which left him feeling very insecure and unloved. You need to understand where he is coming from and help him become responsible, as you have the potential to have a great future together. Talking will be a good start to the healing process.

6. A high flier will enter your life very shortly and sweep you off your feet in a whirlwind romance. You will be reeling with excitement and feel it is all a dream, but it is reality and you deserve it after all the disappointments of the past. Fate is finally smiling on you and you should enjoy what she has to bring.

RING

Like every closed circle the ring is symbolic of continuity and wholeness. It is a symbol therefore of marriage or, at its most basic level, commitment.

1. You are feeling unsure about things and need to take time to think about where you stand. You need to be totally honest with yourself and realise that the hardest part in all of this is making a decision. Make a note of all the pros and cons, then act on it. You will feel a weight lift from your shoulders when you do.

2. Great excitement as you are asked for your hand in marriage. This will come as a total surprise to you, but your lover will have been planning it for weeks. You will delay your answer just to get your breath back. But if you are wise the answer will be a resounding 'yes'!

3. You can't put your finger on it, but there is something missing from your relationship. If you can find this missing spark then things will be fine, but you need to take action immediately before the rot sets in. The ball, as they say, is firmly in your court.

4. Everyone around you seems to be getting married and even people who never seemed to be in relationships are now moving in with partners. You feel as though Fate is making you forever the bridesmaid and never the bride, but this will not be the case in six months' time. Your soul mate is out there, you just have to find him.

5. You are with a commitment phobe. He finds going steady or being in a permanent relationship a scary concept. You

are compatible, though, and all you have to do is build his confidence in the whole concept of partnership. He does love you, so use your feminine charms to make him feel he can't live without you.

6. In the past you have had a broken relationship or marriage which left you emotionally hurt and spiritually damaged. The hurt was deep within your soul. You need to heal your past by accepting what has been and lighting a blue candle to come to terms with all you have been through. Heal your past and your future will be happy, as love and a person who treats you well will be in the picture.

BOOK

A book signifies acquired knowledge and great wisdom. It often relates to a situation where getting help from a wise person will be of benefit. A book can be open, which reveals a person who has emotions on display, or closed, which signifies a person who hides what they are feeling.

1. You have learned a lot from past relationships. There is a common thread and you are not entirely blameless. You need to alter your behaviour so that relationships stand a real chance in the future with you. Emotionally you can be very draining, so learn to share the burden in other ways such as writing things down or getting help from friends.

2. You are a stubborn person and you make things difficult for yourself. An important lesson for you is to compromise in relationships. This will mean that love is able to blossom where disagreements seem to be at present. Compromise is easy, so take heed of this wisdom and just do it.

3. Love is a many-splendoured thing and your inner goddess is telling you that it is within your reach. Listen to her message and light pink candles today in her honour. She is helping to bring love into your life but you must hear her message and act on it. Your life will be filled with good things and people and you deserve this.

4. A wise older person is trying to give you advice, but you may not be listening. They can help you as they have seen it all before. Taking their advice and acting on their wisdom will bring valuable results that will help your love life to stay on track.

5. OK, yours is not a textbook relationship – it is far more exciting than that. You feel a rush of pleasure whenever your special person phones or e-mails you. Go with what feels right, as life will never be dull when this person is around. His novel approach to life will always brighten up the most boring day.

6. For your love life to work you need to ask for help. Luckily you have a great source of inspiration at your very fingertips – your friends. They are amazing and love you very much. They even know many likely candidates who could be the Mr Right you have been seeking. That is, if you haven't found him already.

MOON

The moon symbolises the emotions and she has an effect on all of us as she passes through her 29-day cycle. Without her influence our feelings would be difficult to understand, both for us and for those around us.

1. Now is the time to be upfront about your feelings. Being honest will put you in a much stronger position. Hiding how you feel could mean that you miss out on a golden opportunity for love and romance. The person you are thinking of is not a mind reader, so speak your mind. You will be thrilled with the response you get.

2. You are under the illusion that things are OK in your relationship when they clearly are not. You are not seeing the negative signs as you are closing your eyes to the situation. If you continue to do this, you will only get hurt. If you wake up and smell the coffee, then things can improve for all concerned.

3. Your cup is half full, not half empty. This positive attitude will see you through life. Get out more and enjoy the pleasures that are about to reveal themselves to you. Socialising is the key to your love life, which is set to take off in the most fantastic fashion. No more Saturday nights stuck in front of the telly. There is a whole world waiting for you.

4. You think you have found love and you can't believe your luck, but you have worked hard to feel like this. Enjoy the time you have in this relationship, as love like this only comes around once in a lifetime. Write a note to your lover telling him how you feel. He will appreciate it.

5. Jealousy is limiting your life at present. Don't allow this to happen or you will find that relationships don't work because you are constantly checking on your lover's movements. People need their own space and you just can't allow that because of your green-eyed monster. You

need to look deep within your soul to find why this is the case.

6. It is time to wear your heart on your sleeve. This will get the response you are looking for. A ring will also be given to you as a gift of love. This will make you the happiest person on Earth at the moment. Don't hold back, as your affection will be reciprocated, much to your surprise.

IVY

This is a feminine symbol denoting protection from all evil or outside forces. Ivy ensures that you are secure in your daily life and is a great emblem of hope for the future.

1. You feel as if you are wasting your time and resources at present. In particular a person at work has been making you unhappy and your relationship is under immense strain as a result. You need to think about this before anything else.

2. You are trying your best to keep fit and eat healthily. This will soon go to pot as you are whisked away to a surprise destination. Two crystal champagne glasses, his and hers white cotton bathrobes and chilled strawberries will all be significant. You will think you have died and gone to heaven, and in a way you have. Just enjoy it.

3. You tend to build a wall around yourself. It is your safety mechanism to stop you from getting hurt as you have been in the past. If you keep doing this, though, you will miss out on the most amazing relationships and experiences. Learn to bring down the barriers that rule your life so much on a day-to-day basis.

4. Communication in the form of a letter will bring joy to your heart. It will say so much and a lot of it is what you have been wanting to hear. Perhaps you never expected the writer to feel this way about you. You will realise that he can bring so much vitality to your life. The best advice is to return the compliment and write your own letter. Just speak from the heart.

5. A significant person from your past is very likely to walk back into your life very soon. He has the ability to bring you much joy. The symbol of the crown of state and legal matters will be very significant to him, as will matters of security. Don't allow him to slip through your fingers this time, as he could make your life complete.

6. You feel ugly, fat and fed up just now. You lack confidence, which makes your personal image very negative. Still, you have amazing feminine energy and power. Learning to tap into this will change your view about yourself. On the next Full Moon light a silver candle and ask for inspiration. You will be amazed by the results.

CLOCK

The clock is a symbol of time and also perpetual motion. Time never stands still, but moves at a constant rate, and the clock rules our lives – sometimes a good thing, other times a bad thing.

1. You have waited a long time to feel as you do at this moment. There are lots of fun and frolics still to come and much laughter, with two souls coming together with

the most perfect timing imaginable. Passion and excitement are now a regular occurrence for you. No wonder you are walking around with a big smile on your face.

2. You have a big decision to make, but now is not the right time to make it. Talk it over with the most important woman in your life, your mother figure. Her wisdom will help you to decide when the time is right. The decision is too important just to rush into, but when you make it, it will change the course of your life forever. Ask for help and you will be OK.

3. You are about to enter a period of uncertainty due to someone's lack of clarity. You are a special person and you deserve to be treated as such. Don't ever settle for second fiddle or beg for attention when it should be given freely. A promised phone call which doesn't materialise may be the last straw for you here.

4. Things can't happen quickly enough for you just now. Patience is a virtue but one you do not possess at present. However, don't rush into things just now. Your love life will develop as you desire, but taking your time is key to it being a great success. A change of address and a door with a brass knocker will be significant sooner than you expect.

5. Can your life get any more complicated just now? Work issues and family concerns seem to be putting pressure on a relationship that you are in. You need to take time and look at things from the outside. This perspective will make things easier to handle so that your troubles can be tackled head on.

6. The time has come for you to go on a romantic break. Hills and lakes will be significant, as will the sounds of birds singing. You need time to get away from it all so that you can concentrate on your loved one without interruption. Mobile phones should be shut off for the duration. Getting out into nature will give the relationship chance to ground.

TREE

A tree is a symbol of growth and expansion. It has strong roots that hold it in place and ground it. As a symbol, it indicates change, just as a tree changes through the seasons. It also signifies hard work, as so many factors need to work together for a tree to thrive.

1. You need to push forward on the subject of relationships. You know you are strongly attracted to someone in your work setting and it is now time to act on these feelings. He feels the same way about you, so ask him out for a drink or better still a date. Luck is smiling on you and there is no time to spare.

2. You have major issues surrounding your living space at present. There are parts of your home which really annoy you, as they are not the way you want them. Finances and a lack of time have made change impossible for you. This is making you frustrated and you need to work out how you can make your home a comfortable place for you again. Then you will be easier to get on with.

3. You have many mixed feelings concerning your love life, or the distinct lack of it. You need to ground yourself so

that you can see where you are heading. Light a green candle and imagine that your feet have roots coming from them which hold you in place. Finding the love that you want is not impossible, but take the oracle's advice and ground yourself first.

4. Your horizons are expanding all the time and this may mean that you soon have to consider moving location. Your relationship will survive this, as it is unlikely that a chance like this will come again in your life. This life change will trigger a whole set of opportunities for you and the chance to enjoy the rewards of your hard work in your career and relationships.

5. Better things are to come and an area of training you have been intrigued by will become significant in your life. Your love life will improve as you expand your knowledge and horizons. The training will also result in you becoming a happier, more rounded person and there will be a blue certificate at the end of it.

6. You are worried that your relationship is unsettled just now. You may feel that your partner is looking elsewhere for excitement – the excitement that you once had. Don't give up, fight for what you had. You can get the spark back. Learning the art of Tantric sex will be a great way to bring the thrill back.

ROSE

A rose is a symbol of completion and perfection. It is the flower of lovers and a red rose reveals everlasting love. But roses do have thorns, so you do have to be careful when handling them.

1. Have a cosy night in with your lover. Sit and watch a soppy video, have a takeaway and a bottle of wine. Make sure there are plenty of cuddles and kisses. There should be no pressure, just a night slobbing about. Sometimes this closeness is just enough to make you feel connected to your special person.

2. You do have a happy relationship which makes you feel content, so tell your partner that you love him. He needs to hear those words just now, as he feels insecure in his career. Romantic gestures like letters or small gifts will also help him feel wanted at this difficult time for him.

3. Your inner goddess is trying to give you advice concerning your love life. Why aren't you listening to her wisdom? She can help you have a fulfilled and contented life, and sexually she will help reignite your libido, as it has diminished somewhat recently.

4. A stranger with green eyes will bring powerful positive changes to your life. It is time that you stopped thinking about what other people think and did what your gut instinct is telling you. You can experience a whole new world which has eluded you up to now.

5. A friend will phone you for advice. She has been there to help you at difficult points in your life, it is now time for you to help her. You may have to travel to see her and offer your support first hand. If you are in a relationship, you need to explain why you are doing this, as otherwise your partner may seem uncaring and obstructive.

6. You are lucky to have a person in your life who treats you like a goddess. He will send you flowers and write you poems on a regular basis. You have truly met your knight in shining armour, but never take him for granted, as he needs to be cared for too. His past will make him need attention and mothering.

CANDLE

A candle is a symbol of hope, as it brings light into a situation. It also burns fire, which is one of the four elements. Without heat we could not survive. A single candle can also be a symbol of love for those souls that we have lost.

1. The past two months have been difficult for you. Your work has seemed out of control due to mismanagement and your relationships have suffered as a consequence. You are going to enter a more positive and productive period very soon. There will also be a change of staff and management which will bring a smile to your face and to those of many colleagues.

2. The person you love needs your support. He has had a loss which has affected him much more than he would like people to know. He feels isolated and needs to know that you are there for him. Legal matters will also be at the forefront of his mind and you need him to keep focused to gain a positive result in this respect.

3. A fountain and the opera will be significant to you. A romantic break will light up your life and a proposal will surprise you. You will say yes and this will lead to the happiest if not busiest time of your life to date. You will

love the organising and planning. Enjoy this time, as it will be very special.

4. It is time for you to nourish your body and soul. Eat a balanced diet and drink plenty of water. You feel that you are ageing and this could be down to the stressful six months you have just lived through. Turn over a new leaf and get a gym membership, one that you use this time! A healthier diet will also help you feel better and your relationship will benefit as a result.

5. Don't allow others to put you off your crusade. The person you love may not be cooperating as you would wish and friends may feel that your efforts are fruitless, but the oracle tells you not to give up the fight. You just don't understand where he is coming from.

6. You are at a crossroads in your life and this includes your career, love life and home situation. Change will only come once you decide what you really want. You need time on your own just to meditate and ask for guidance. The answers will come to you in the form of dreams, so make note of all the dreams you have.

RAINBOW

A rainbow is seen in a clear bright sky when there is rain about. It is an arc of the most beautiful colours and a lucky omen. According to Irish folklore there is a crock of gold at the end of it.

1. Your luck is finally changing for the better. Many obstacles that have been in your way are now merely

stepping-stones you can cross. A wish you make on Thursday will come true right in front of your eyes. Make sure you know exactly what to wish for, as luck like this doesn't come around every day but every decade.

2. A small child who is likely to be a member of your family will be celebrating a very important event soon and you will see your lover in a whole new light as he has a real ability to relate to children. This will only add to the charisma that he already has in bundles. Just remember that children are magical and can bring so much fulfilment to life.

3. Communication is the key to your relationship running smoothly. When people fail to talk about their worries, concerns and troubles, that is when barriers build up. Go out for a nice dinner at a quiet restaurant so you can say your piece. You will feel better for it, as will your lover, as he has been feeling the same. Good food and good conversation are key to a good relationship.

4. You are considering a holiday at the moment. The oracle sees a place steeped in history and a beautiful cathedral with stained glass as being significant. There will also be a map showing where a set of ruins is that you will have a great interest in. Romance could come to you on this holiday if it is not currently in your life. If it is, then you may meet someone else who sweeps you off your feet.

5. Count your blessings as a colleague you have had difficulty with in the past will leave your place of work and you will receive the offer of a promotion that will be

music to your ears. The increased workload will play havoc with your social and love life, though, so be warned.

6. A sporting occasion where a brightly coloured flag is flown will give your love life a welcome boost. Just enjoy the free booze and food on offer and drop your inhibitions. This will be good for you, as you can finally get the attention you deserve and at times you can be too serious and retentive. Go on, live a little – you won't have any regrets.

I have enjoyed writing this book, as love is my favourite subject in the whole wide universe. I hope you have relished it too and will have fun and great journeys working through it. Who knows, you may meet your Prince Charming using a little bit of Ruth the Truth magic. Please let me know how you get on. Any queries or questions, please write to me at:

Ruth Urquhart
Psychic Services
Millworks
Field Road
Busby
Glasgow G76 8SE

Ruth the Truth's Psychic Guide, also published by Piatkus, was Ruth Urquhart's first book. In it she examines all aspects of life – including love and relationships, career and finances, and health – and explains how to unlock the psychic potential that lies within you.

Available in paperback at all good bookshops, price £8.99 (ISBN: 0 7499 22338).

Resources

I particularly like using the following magical resources to work my own magic and rituals. I am sure you will find them fantastic too.

Clearly Natural
PO Box 4, Camberley, Surrey, GU15 2YY; Telephone: 01276 675609
This small business was the brainchild of Sarah Ropella and provides a complete range of natural vegetable-based and organic toiletries. I use the Provençal breeze soap in my bath, which has lavender to help me relax. As a mail-order company you will find their service swift and thorough.

Pure Scents
13 Dogpole, Shrewsbury, Shropshire, SY1 1EN; Telephone: 01743 356677
This small, family-run business makes the most natural and wholesome health and beauty products. To get the full benefits on my section on stress relief you should try their geranium and rosewood bath oil. They have a mail order service, so no matter where you live they are never far away.

Raven
17 Melton Fields, Brickyard Lane, North Ferriby, East Yorks., HU4 3HE; Telephone: 01482 632512
This is a small mail-order company which stocks all of the weird and wonderful things I mention in the book, including crystals, herbs, oils and jewellery. I use them all the time and the owners, Chris and Graham, have a friendly approach if you need any help.

INDEX

Page numbers in **bold** refer to diagrams. Page numbers in *italics* refer to tables.

Index

If you have enjoyed this book you might be interested in the following titles, also published by Piatkus.

Anand, Margot, *The Art of Sexual Magic*

Borysenko, Joan, *A Woman's Spiritual Journey*

Bowes, Sue, *Woman's Magic*

Bradshaw, John, *Creating Love*

Choquette, Sonia, *Your Heart's Desire*

Ciaramicoli, Arthur, *The Power of Empathy*

Cooper, Diana, *Light Up Your Life*

Cooper, Diana, *Transform Your Life*

Eason, Cassandra, *A Magical Guide to Love and Sex*

Evans, Sybil, with Suib Cohen, Sherry, *Hot Buttons*

Glass, Dr. Lillian, *He Says, She Says*

Ivens, Sarah, *A Modern Girl's Guide to Getting Hitched*

Jeffers, Susan, *Dare to Connect*

Lerner, Harriet, *The Dance of Connection*

O'Neil, Janet, *Cracking the Love Code*

Ovenstein, Peggy, *Women on Work, Love, Children and Life*

Page, Susan, *If We're So In Love Why Aren't We Happy*

Paget, Lou, *How to be a Great Lover*

Peiffer, Vera, *Inner Happiness*

Peiffer, Vera, *Positive Living*

Shapiro, Debbie, *Your Body Speaks Your Mind*

Simpson, Liz, *Finding Fulfilment*

Stern, Malcolm and Bristow, Sujata, *The Courage to Love*

Weis, Dr. Brian, *Only Love is Real*

Young-Eisendrath, Polly, *Women and Desire*